IP Routing Protocols Workbook

Prepared and presented by

UYLESS BLACK

Pearson PTR Interactive
Internet Telephony Video Course

Prentice Hall PTR
Upper Saddle River, New Jersey 07458

Table of Contents

LECTURE 1   Getting Started   1

LECTURE 2   IP Routing Introduction   17

LECTURE 3   Bridges, Routers, and Gateways   33

LECTURE 4   Minimum Hop Protocols   47

LECTURE 5   Link State Metric Protocols   57

LECTURE 6   LAN Bridges   73

LECTURE 7   IP Routing Protocols in Action   89

LECTURE 8   Network Address Translation (NAT)   101

LECTURE 9   Major Attributes of the Protocols   113

LECTURE 10   RIP Basics   123

LECTURE 11   RIP Operations   137

LECTURE 12   MPLS and Label Distribution   149

LECTURE 13   OSPF Basics   165

LECTURE 14   OSPF Operations   187

LECTURE 15   IS-IS (Intermediate System-to-Intermediate
             System)   201

LECTURE 16   BGP Basics   211

LECTURE 17   BGP Operations   225

LECTURE 18   PNNI   239

LECTURE 19   Routing in Mobile Networks   249

LECTURE 20   Wrap-Up   269

Welcome to the Pearson PTR Interactive Internet Telephony Video Course. Before we get started, we need to discuss a few matters pertaining to this course. First, we will take you through the major topics and objectives for the course.

Next, the Pearson Advanced Communications Technologies Series is explained, followed by a description of how this video training fits into the overall curriculum.

The organization of the course material is discussed, with a brief explanation of each module (lesson) in the course.

I will explain the approach to the course presentation and introduce you to the format and style of the course material.

Lastly, the Web page references for this course will be provided for you to use as additional learning tools, and as follow-up material to this course.

Lecture 1

Getting Started

Major Topics

- Major Topics/Objectives

- The Advanced Communications Technologies Series

- Organization of the course material

- Approach to the course presentation

- Web page references

The short list on the right side of the page states the objectives for this training class. As you can see, they are short, but they will entail considerable analysis and effort. However, we have laid out the course and material to make the process effective.

<u>Objectives</u>

- Achieve a strong foundation in IP Routing Protocols

- Understand the trade-offs of various approaches

- Become familiar with the Internet Routing Standards

Notes:

_____

_____

_____

_____

_____

_____

This chart depicts the Uyless Black Advanced Communications Technologies Series organization. Each of these titles represents a book, and the shaded boxes represent books that will be published in the future.

This course is organized around the text *IP Routing Protocols*. And the course material you have in front of you includes this book.

The structure of the chart shows (in a general fashion) the interrelationships of the books. The horizontal and vertical lines convey how certain books in the series should be read before others.

However, be aware that each book is a stand-alone topic. If certain topics are prerequisites to a book, extractions are taken from the prerequisite book and offered to the reader in an appendix. In this manner, you do not have to buy the prerequisite book unless you want more information on the topic.

The Advanced Communications Technologies Series

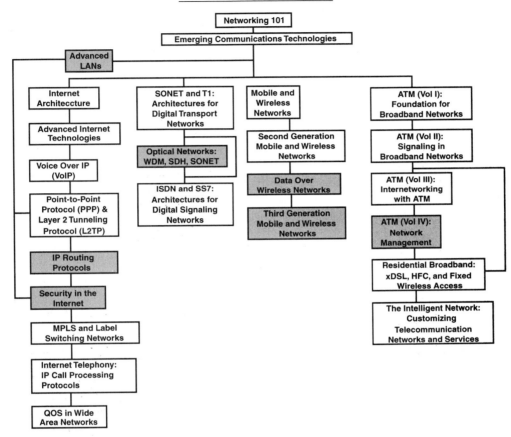

Shaded boxes are books under development

Notes:

_____

_____

_____

_____

This chart shows the tactical plan for the Pearson PTR Interactive Video Courses. These four courses will be developed and produced in 2000. As you can see, the emphasis in the initial courses revolves around the Internet. As the series evolves, other important topics will be added to the curriculum.

Internet Video Training Series for 2000

- Internet Architecture and Protocols

- IP Telephony

- Routing and Switching

- Title # 4: TBD (To be determined)

Notes:

_____

_____

_____

_____

_____

_____

The prerequisite for this training is the Internet Architecture and Protocols video class.

Prerequisite for this Training

The Internet Architecture
An Introduction to IP Protocols

And in the IP Routing Protocols book:
Chapter 2 and the first three appendices

Notes:

_____

_____

_____

_____

_____

_____

The course is organized into twenty modules or lessons. They are listed in this figure. We review them briefly now, and of course delve into them in more detail as we proceed through the course.

IP Routing Protocols
Organization of Course Material

1. Getting started
2. IP Routing Introduction
3. Bridges, Routers, and Gateways
4. Minimum Hop Protocols
5. Link State Metric Protocols
6. LAN Bridges
7. IP Routing Protocols in Action
8. Network Address Translation (NAT)
9. Major Attributes of the Protocols
10. RIP Basics
11. RIP Operations
12. MPLS and Label Distribution
13. OSPF Basics
14. OSPF Operations
15. IS-IS
16. BGP Basics
17. BGP Operations
18. PNNI
19. Routing in Mobile Networks
20. Wrap-up

Notes:

_____

_____

_____

_____

_____

The course material has been designed to provide you with the tools to: (a) learn about the subject during the video presentations by using the workbook reference manual, (b) amplify this learning by reading the enclosed textbook, and (c) access the Web for questions and answers, as well as follow up information from your instructor.

You will find the workbook reference manual of great help during the lectures. It reflects the major parts of the textbook but has been designed to assist you in assimilating the lecture material.

Approach to the Course Presentation

- Workbook: Designed for your work with the video

   Text on left page amplifies graphics/tables on right page

- Textbook: Designed for follow up reading

- Animations provided to enhanced learning process

- Web pages for follow ups to course presentation

- Questions and answers are available on the Web

Notes:

_____

_____

_____

_____

_____

This Web site is the anchor point for your work with this course. Here you will find the questions and answers to the exercises for the course, as well as any follow-ups to the course, such as papers on the subject.

Web References

- Go to this Web site for all references to the Uyless Black Internet Curriculum:

  www.phptr.com/black

Notes:

_____

_____

_____

_____

_____

Lecture 2

IP Routing
Introduction

Major Topics

- Functions of routing protocols

- Routing domains

- Routing vs. forwarding

- Types of route advertisements

The functions of routing protocols are really quite simple. These protocols advertise IP addresses. These addresses are assigned to IP nodes, such as personal computers, routers, name servers, and security access servers. These advertisements are very important. Without them, we Internet users would not be able to send e-mail and files to our business associates, friends, and relatives, all of whom are identified with an Internet address.

The task of the routing protocol is to find a "best" path to the computers that are located at these addresses. The term *best* is relative to what the network administrator considers important, as well as to what the routing protocol can support. Best might be a path with the fewest number of hops (intermediate nodes, such as routers) between the sender and receiver of the traffic. It might be a path that exhibits the highest throughput, measured in bit/s. We will see that some of the routing protocols discussed in this course are designed to support specific implementations of a "best" path.

IP uses a routing table to make forwarding decisions on IP traffic. The routing protocols provide a means to build the routing tables for IP to use to forward traffic to destination addresses and, therefore, to the destination user.

Functions of IP Routing Protocols

- Advertise IP addresses

- Find "best" path to computers at the addresses

- Provide a means to build routing tables …

- … For IP to use to forward traffic to IP addresses

Notes:

_____

_____

_____

_____

_____

_____

A key concept for this seminar is the concept of a routing domain. The routing domain is an administrative entity, and its scope depends on the decisions of the network manager. The term *scope* means how many networks are associated with the domain. A small domain consists of a few networks; a large domain consists of many. The size of the routing domain is relative, but its goal is to establish boundaries for the dissemination of routing information. If the domain contains many networks, it is likely that more route advertisements must be exchanged than in a domain with fewer networks.

In addition, a routing domain is useful for security administration. For example, an organization's routing domain may consist of trusted networks, in which limited security procedures are implemented. Then at the edges of the routing domain are firewalls that filter traffic into and out of the domain. In fact, the security policy of the routing domain may forbid the passing through of certain traffic.

Another function of the routing domain is for accounting, billing, and revenue purposes. Obviously, if the network manager cannot control his/her domain and account for traffic, it is impossible to know how to charge for a service.

This figure shows how the components may be configured inside the domain. In most situations, a router acts as the conduit of traffic into and out of the domain. In addition, the router acts as the conduit for the passing and reception of route advertising information.

In many situations, a designated router is assigned the task of route advertising and if more than one router is attached to the network, one of them is designated as the primary router.

The Routing Domain

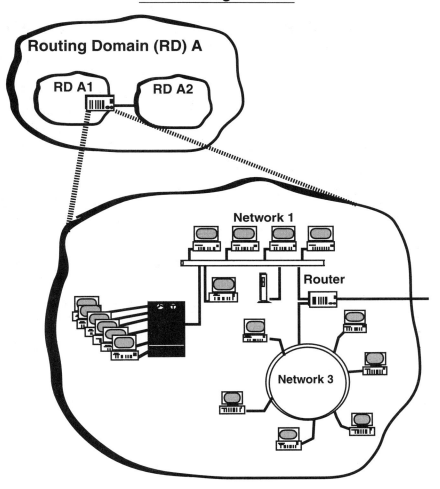

Notes:

_____

_____

_____

_____

In the Internet or in intranets, it is a common approach to establish hierarchies of routing domains (levels of domains). In this figure, two routing domains are connected, RDA and RDB. The two routers in these domains have been configured to be domain border routers; they are responsible for the exchange of routing information on behalf of their respective routing domains.

The hierarchy in this figure is as follows: RDA is divided into two other routing domains, RDA1 and RDA2. Likewise, RDB is divided into two other routing domains, RDB1 and RDB2. Each of these four "subdomains" also has a designated router (or routers) that is (are) responsible for route advertising into and out of the domains.

One attractive aspect of the hierarchical approach to internetworking is the practice of using routing domains to do summary or aggregated advertising. For example, the router at RDA1 can use network masks or address prefixes to advertise multiple hosts and subnets within the domain.

These last two figures are generic in nature, and I have described general concepts so far. We will delve into considerable detail later, and we will introduce more specific terms.

Connecting High-level
Routing Domains (RD)

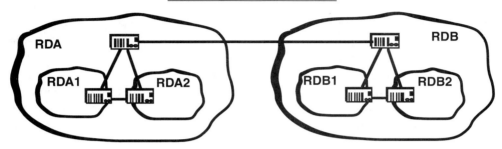

Notes:

_____

_____

_____

_____

_____

_____

Before proceeding further, it is a good idea to clarify some terms. In the past, the term *routing* referred to operations in which packets were relayed through a node from an incoming interface to an outgoing interface. The relaying occurred by matching the destination address in the incoming packet with a routing table entry. If a match occurred, the table revealed the next node to receive the packet (if appropriate) and the associated output interface.

These same operations are still in place today, but the term *routing* is usually not employed. Instead the term *forwarding* is used. Be aware that some documents still use the term *routing* to describe these operations.

So, what does *routing* mean in more current context? It refers to the process of route advertising/route discovery.

Therefore, two protocols are involved in the internetworking process:

- **Forwarding:** Using a routing table to make a forwarding decision
- **Routing:** Using route advertisements to acquire the knowledge to create the routing table that the forwarding protocol uses

Another point about the creation of the routing table: It need not be created with the routing protocol. In some situations, entries in the table can be manually configured, and in others, the entries are created with other protocols, such as the Address Resolution Protocol (ARP).

Routing and Forwarding

- Routing
    1. Using route advertisements
    2. To acquire the knowledge
    3. To create the routing table that…
    4. The forwarding protocol uses

- Forwarding
    1. Using the routing table
    2. To make a forwarding decision

And Sources of Routing Information

- Directly connected to common network:
  an address resolution protocol
- Static route (manually configured)
- A routing protocol

Notes:

_____

_____

_____

_____

_____

_____

This figure is an example of a routing table found in a router. Individual systems differ in the contents of the routing table, but they all resemble this example. Some tables may have more entries, but most have fewer. The entries in the table are:

- **Destination:** IP address of the destination node.
- **Route Mask:** Mask that is used with the destination address to identify bits that are used in routing. Newer systems use a prefix that accomplishes the same function.
- **Next Hop:** IP address of the next hop in the route.
- **If Index (port):** Physical port (interface) on the router to reach the next hop address.
- **Metric/Admin Distance:** "Cost" to reach the destination address, and the admin distance (a value that assesses the trustworthiness of the information).
- **Route Type:** Directly attached to the router (direct), or reached through another router (remote).
- **Source of Route:** How the route was discovered.
- **Route Age:** Number of seconds since the route was last updated.
- **Route Information:** Miscellaneous information.
- **MTU:** Maximum transmission unit size (size of the L_2 data field).

Typical Routing Table

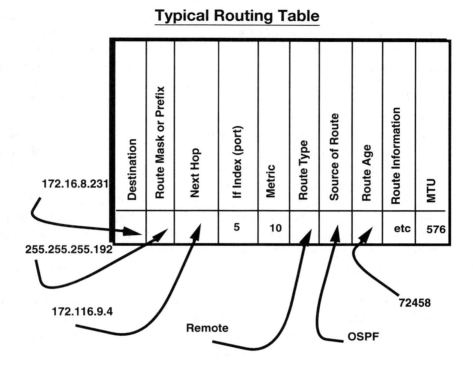

Where:
MTU   Maximum transmission unit size (in bytes, of the L_2 I field)

There are two types of route advertising protocols used in the data communications industry: (a) distance-vector and (b) link state metric.

The distance-vector protocol is more commonly known as a minimum hop protocol, which means the protocol searches for a path between a sending and receiving machine that has the fewest number of intermediate machines (hops) between them. The term *distance* refers to the number of hops to a "vector" (an address).

Each router calculating a best path (fewest hops) to a destination implements the minimum hop approach, and if certain conditions change, the router advertises this change to its neighbor(s), which results in each neighbor changing its routing table.

The link state metric protocol assigns a value (metric) to each link in the system. Each node advertises its links by sending messages to its neighbors. These messages contain the link's metric (or metrics, if advertising is done on more than one metric criterion). The path chosen between the machines is the one in which the metrics of all the links making up the path are summed to a lower value than any other contending path.

The link state approach is implemented by each router using the same copy of a database (a replicated distributed file at each router). Each router plays a part in the creation of this database by sending to all routers in the routing domain information on the router's active links to its local networks and to other routers. The accompanying metric becomes part of the database, which is used to compute the routes.

Route Advertising

Types of Route Advertising:

- Distance-vector (Minimum hop)
    Route between sending and receiving machine:
        Fewest number of intermediate hops

- Link state metric
    Route between sending and receiving machine:
        Sum of path "metrics" is smallest

Notes:

_____

_____

_____

_____

_____

_____

Notes:

_____

_____

_____

_____

_____

_____

Summary

- Routing protocols discover:
  IP addresses and,
  the "best" paths to those addresses

- Routing protocols are organized around:
  Routing domains, in order to:
     1. Contain the number of routing messages
     2. Control the domain

Lecture 3

Bridges, Routers, and Gateways

Major Topics

- Comparison of bridges, routers and gateways

- Where these units are placed in the Internet Model

- Stub, default, and static routes

Networks were originally conceived to be fairly small systems consisting of relatively few machines. As the need for data communications services has grown, it has become necessary to connect networks together for the sharing of resources, distribution of functions, and administrative control. In addition, some LANs, by virtue of their restricted distance, often need to be connected together through other devices, such as bridges and routers.

This figure shows the relationships of these devices vis-à-vis a layered model. A *repeater* is used to connect the media on a LAN, typically called *media segments*. The repeater has no upper-layer functions; its principal job is to terminate the signal on one LAN segment and regenerate it on another LAN segment.

The *bridge* operates at the data link layer (always at the Media Access Control [MAC] sublayer and sometimes at the Logical Link Control [LLC] sublayer). Typically, it uses MAC physical addresses to perform its relaying functions. As a general rule, it is a fairly low-function device and connects networks that are homogeneous (for example, IEEE-based networks).

A *router* operates at the network layer because it uses network layer addresses (for example: IP, X.121, E.164 addresses). It usually contains more capabilities than a bridge and may offer flow control mechanisms as well as source routing or non-source routing features.

The term *gateway* is used to describe an entity (a machine or software module) that may perform routing capabilities and also may act as a protocol conversion or mapping facility. For example, such a gateway could relay traffic and also provide conversion between two different types of mail transfer applications.

To avoid any confusion about these terms, some people use the term *internetworking unit (IWU)*. IWU is a generic term to describe a router, gateway, bridge, or anything else that performs relaying functions between networks.

"Routing/Bridging/Gateway" Protocols

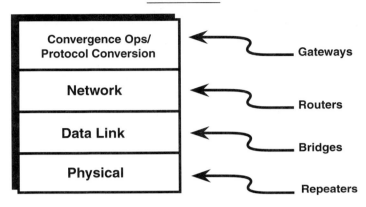

Notes:

_____

_____

_____

_____

_____

_____

Route discovery can take place with layer 2 or layer 3 addresses. This section goes into more detail about the layered model and the placement of protocols in the protocol stack. This figure shows the placement of route discovery protocols in the Internet layered architecture that pertain to layer 2 or layer 3 route discovery protocols.

First, in Figure (a), the general Internet layered model is shown. This model and the functions of the layers are described later. Next, the bridge model is shown in Figure (b). Recall that the bridge operates at the data link layer, with MAC addresses, and is designed to internetwork LANs.

Our focus is now on Figure (c). The routing protocols operate in this model in three "layered positions." First, some of the protocols operate without layer 4 (TCP or UDP) and are positioned in this figure running on top of IP, IPX, etc. Second, others run over TCP, and third, others run over UDP.

Protocol Placements in the Internet Layered Model

| Application   Layer (L_7) |
| Transport   Layer (L_4) |
| Network Layer (L_3) |
| Data Link Layer (L_2) |
| Physical Layer (L_1) |

(a) The Layered Model

| Routing |
| Physical Layer (L_1) |

(b) The Bridge Model

	Routing	Routing
Routing	TCP	UDP
IP, IPX, etc. (L_3)		
Data Link Layer (L_2)		
Physical Layer (L_1)		

(c) The Router Model

Notes:

_____

_____

_____

_____

_____

Bridges are designed to interconnect LANs; therefore, it is convenient for them to use a MAC address in determining how to relay the traffic between LANs. Additionally, a bridge "pushes" the conventional network layer responsibilities of route discovery and relaying operations into the data link layer. In effect, a bridge has no conventional network layer. Bridges may also implement the SPF, which was just discussed.

This example shows a multiport bridge, which accepts a frame coming in on a port from network A. The frame is examined by the MAC relay entity, and a decision is made to relay the traffic on an output port to network C.

By virtue of the design of a bridge (no technical reason exists why a bridge could not exhibit more functionality), it has relatively limited buffering capability. Also, there is no provision for data integrity in bridges (such as the acknowledgment of traffic, and the possible retransmission of erred traffic). As a consequence, frames can be discarded if the bridge becomes congested. On the other hand, bridges are fast, and they are very easy to implement. Indeed, most bridges are self-configuring. This feature relieves network managers of many onerous tasks, such as constant management of a number of naming and network reconfiguration parameters.

Bridge Operations

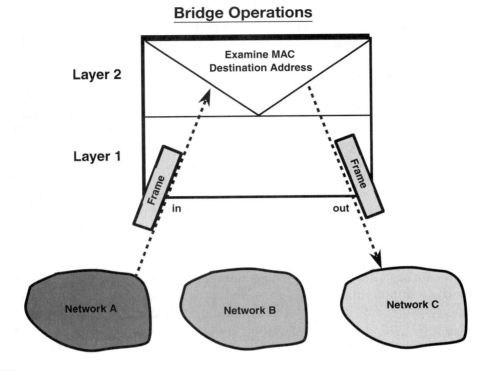

Where:
  MAC   Media access control (a LAN address)

Notes:

_____

_____

_____

_____

_____

_____

While the definition of routers varies in the industry, the majority of people define a router as a machine that performs operations at the network layer. Therefore, routers use conventional network addresses such as X.121, IP, an SNA network address, an OSI address, etc.

Routers can use the same type of route discovery and relay operations as a bridge. Indeed, many routers and bridges use the same type of operation to determine how to route traffic to the next network. As examples, spanning tree operations and source routing can be used at either the data link or the network layer.

Therefore, other than addressing, what is the difference between a router and a bridge, and why should there be options to use one or the other? A bridge is designed for fewer functions than a conventional router. A router typically allows multiple network protocols to run on the machine. As examples, AppleTalk, DECnet IV, IP, and IPX are commonly supported in routers, and they are usually given a wide variety of options.

In contrast, since a bridge does not use the network layer, it does not have the components to configure and provide options for the network layer protocols. Additionally, bridges have been designed to support the internetworking of LANs only. Consequently, the use of a MAC layer and the MAC relay entity is consistent with LAN architecture. The MAC relay entity can be implemented in hardware, which makes bridge operations efficient and fast.

In contrast, routers are implemented with extensive software modules and provide more extensive value-added features than bridges. Their software orientation also makes them more flexible than bridges. Newer routers are executing routing in hardware with high-speed cache, applications-specific integrated circuits (ASICs), etc.

Router Operations

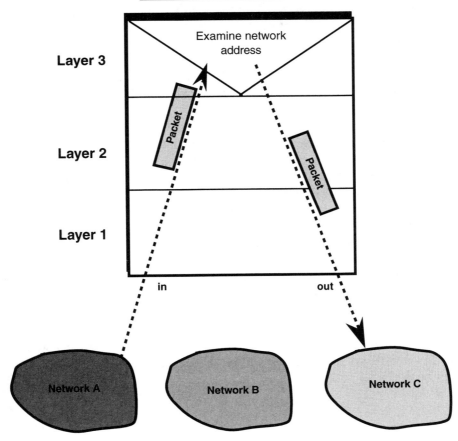

Note: Some machines can route at the data link or network layers

Notes:

_____

_____

_____

_____

Static routes are those that are manually configured. They are entered into the router or bridge tables with configuration commands. A network does not have to have any routes other than static routes, although some implementations do not provide an alternative static route if the primary route fails. But others do, and they are effective for certain situations. One attraction is that they do not require running a routing protocol, and thus do not consume resources for advertising and routing table maintenance.

Static routes are often applied to stub networks. A stub network is one in which traffic emanates or terminates, but traffic does not pass through. Think of a stub network like the end-of-the-line on a subway, or a dead-end street. A stub network can be entered and exited through a static route. Its exit may point to a pre-configured router.

A variation of the static route is the interface static route. For example, assume a network is not directly attached to the interface of a router. Nonetheless, the router can be configured so that the destination address to this network appears to be connected to one of the router's interfaces. This configuration is accomplished by using an administrative distance of zero; of course, this gives the interface precedence over others.

A default route is one that is used as a last resort, after the routing table has been examined and no match can be found for the destination address. It is called the *gateway of last resort* in some literature. Default routes are often used in stub networks, once again, to obviate a routing protocol.

Stubs, Static and Default Routes

(a) "End-of-the-line":

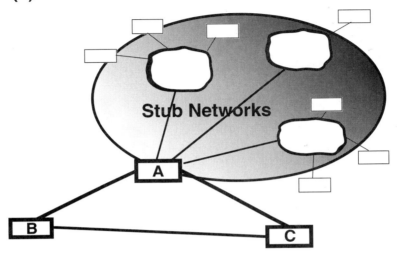

(b) No routing protocol needed:

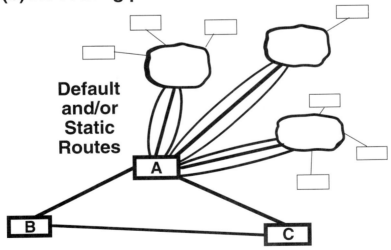

Notes:

_____

_____

_____

_____

_____

_____

Summary

- Bridges, routers and gateways are the key internetworking units in internets

- They run over:
  IP, UDP, or TCP

- Stub, default, and static routes are used often

Lecture 4

Minimum Hop Protocols

Major Topics

- Key operations

- Distribution of routing information

Distance vector protocols use *distributed computation*, which means each router calculates its "best" path to a destination separately from other routers. Each router notifies its neighbors of its known best path, and at the same time, these routers are also notifying their neighbors of their knowledge of the best path.

So, a router obtains information from its neighbors, which may reveal a better path to a destination. In this case, the router updates its table, and also notifies its neighbors of its new choice. This process is iterative, and continues until the routes in the routing domain stabilize.

Distance vector protocols are simple to install, maintain, and troubleshoot. They support address aggregation, and they allow a network administrator to set routing policies, if the administrator so chooses.

Since the advertising through a routing domain occurs in an iterative fashion, and the new route eventually snowballs through the domain, it may take a while for the best routes to be made known to all. For simple distance vector protocols, the size of the routing domain, and the number of hops through it, are usually restricted to a small number. We will later see some examples to reinforce these points.

Basics of Distance Vector Protocols

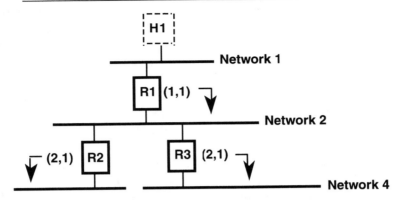

- Each router (e.g., R1):

- Has best path to destination (H1)

- Informs its neighbors (R2 and R3) of path:
  (1,1) = One hop to host 1

Notes:

_____

_____

_____

_____

_____

_____

Distance vector operations rely on each neighbor informing its neighbor(s) about its knowledge of the topology of downstream or upstream nodes. In this example, F informs E that it is directly attached to G on the same network. Since E is aware that it is next to G, it informs C that it is one hop away from G. (Note: some protocols use 0 as directly attached; others use 1.)

C then knows that it is two hops away from G and so C informs A. Since A knows that it is one hop away from C, and has received an advertisement of C's two hops to G, A can infer that it is three hops away from G.

The advertisements of D and B also reach A. It is not unusual for a node to receive multiple advertisements about an address. A makes a comparison of the two alternative routes (one through C and one through B). Obviously A would make the choice using C, since B's advertisements would reveal that it is more hops away from G.

Exchanging Information: Minimum Hop

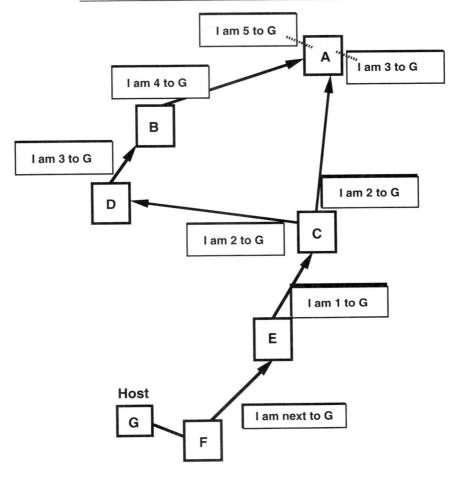

Notes:

_____

_____

_____

_____

This figure shows the result of the route advertisement operation in the previous example. The routing table at node A has been updated to reflect the route to G. (The dashes in the entries in the table are values that are not pertinent to this example.)

The next node to node G is node C, because it is closer to the destination address than the alternative, node B. Once again, closer in this context means the number of hops between the sender and the receiver.

This example shows one entry in the routing table as a result of the advertisement. It is possible to also store the information about next node B, as a secondary route. In the event that problems arise between nodes A and C, the alternative route to G, through B, is already stored in the routing table.

Result of the Route Advertisement

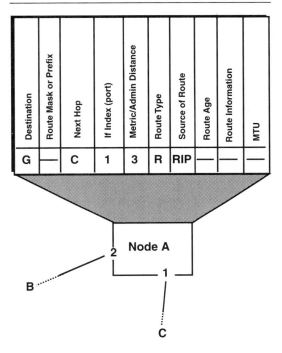

Notes:

_____

_____

_____

_____

_____

_____

Notes:

_____

_____

_____

_____

_____

_____

Summary

- Minimum hop protocols look for a route between sender and receiver:

- ...with the fewest number of hops in between them

- They are also called Distance/Vector protocols

Lecture 5

Link State
Metric Protocols

Major Topics

- Key operations

- Distribution of routing information

- Spanning tree operations

The link state protocol is implemented when a router advertises the state of its local interfaces to its neighbor routers. The local interfaces are the physical links attached to the router. The neighbor router can be a router on the same subnetwork, or on the other end of a point-to-point connection.

Each link interface is assigned a value, also called a metric or a cost. In this figure, router 1 (R1) is advertising a metric of 2 for interface 1, and a metric of 5 for interface 2.

The advertisements are distributed to all routers in the routing domain. The advertisements are used by the routers to learn about the topology of the domain—that is, who is connected to whom, and at what cost.

Although not shown in the figure, router 2 (R2) and router 3 (R3) perform the same operation as router 1. Their metric on the network 2 interface will usually be 5, the same as router 1. The rules for this metric (same or different) depend on the specific routing protocol and the configuration options of the router.

The distribution of the routing information is used to create a database reflecting the topology of the domain. The information in the database is used for route calculations and the construction of a routing table.

Basics of Link-State Protocols

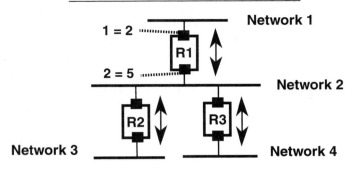

■   = Interfaces (ifIndex)

- Each router:

  Advertises state of its local interfaces

  ... to hosts, other routers, etc.

  Each link assigned a metric (cost)
    e.g. R1: Interface 1 = 2; Interface 2 = 5

- Advertisements distributed to all routers

- ... to create a data base for route calculations

Notes:

_____

_____

_____

_____

_____

_____

The link state metric approach is shown in this figure. Note that node A continues to receive two advertisements about host G. These advertisements contain the sum of the metrics associated with each link connected to the nodes that created the advertisements. The single advertisement begins with node F advertising a "distance" of 2 to host G. This advertisement is conveyed to node E. Previously, nodes F and E have ascertained that the link state metric on the link between them has a value of 1. Consequently, node E adds 1 to the value of 2 it received from node F's advertisement, and creates a route advertisement message to send to node C. Since this advertisement is transmitted across the link between nodes E and C, node C adds the metric associated with this link to the advertised value of 3 coming from E and creates two advertising messages. One message is sent to node A and the other is sent to node D.

The messages find their way to node A, where the final link state sum is 10 on one path and 9 on the other. Consequently, if node A receives traffic destined for host G, it will relay this traffic to node B. Even though C represents the shortest path in number of hops, the path emanating from node B represents the shortest path in relation to the metric count. This situation can occur if (for example) the link between nodes C and A is congested or operating at lesser capacity than the links on the alternate path.

Exchanging Information: Link State Metrics

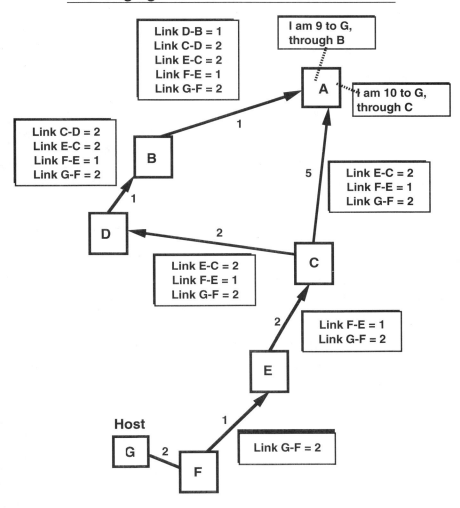

Notes:

_____

_____

_____

In many systems, the industry has moved to the use of link-state protocols, known generally as a shortest path protocol (SPP). The term is inaccurate; a better term is *optimum path,* but the former term is now accepted. These protocols are based on well-tested techniques that have been used in the industry for a number of years.

In this section, we first describe these techniques. Later, we examine how bridges and routers use the SPF techniques. The term *node* in this discussion is synonymous with bridge, gateway, and router.

Ideally, data communications networks are designed to route user traffic based on a variety of criteria, generally referred to as least-cost routing or cost metrics. The name does not mean that routing is based solely on obtaining the least-cost route in the literal sense. Other factors are often part of a network routing algorithm, and are summarized in this figure.

Even though networks vary in least-cost criteria, three constraints must be considered: (a) delay, (b) throughput, and (c) connectivity. If delay is excessive or if throughput is too little, the network does not meet the needs of the user community. The third constraint is quite obvious: the routers and networks must be able to reach each other; otherwise, all other least-cost criteria are irrelevant.

This figure shows the topological database (also called a link-state database) that each node has for its routing domain. Remember that each router has complete information about all other routers. The bridges in a LAN operate the same way.

The Link State Database

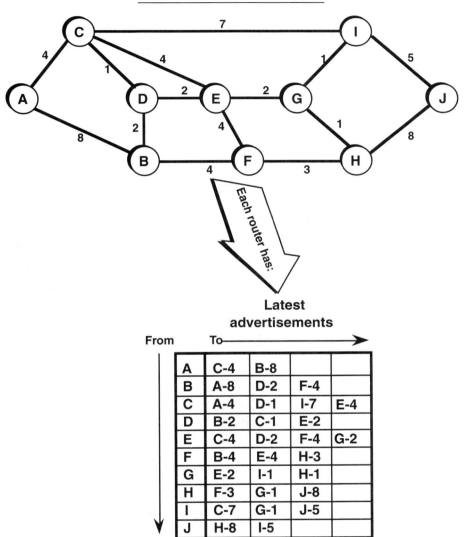

Latest
advertisements

From	To─────────────────────────────▶			
A	C-4	B-8		
B	A-8	D-2	F-4	
C	A-4	D-1	I-7	E-4
D	B-2	C-1	E-2	
E	C-4	D-2	F-4	G-2
F	B-4	E-4	H-3	
G	E-2	I-1	H-1	
H	F-3	G-1	J-8	
I	C-7	G-1	J-5	
J	H-8	I-5		

Notes:

_____

_____

Several shortest-path algorithms are used in the industry. Most of them are based on what is called algorithm A. It is used as the model for the newer internet SPF protocols and has been used for several years to establish optimum designs and network topologies. The concepts discussed here are from "A Note on Two Problems in Connection of Graphs," by E. Dijkstra, *Numerical Mathematics*, October, 1959; *The Design and Analysis of Computer Algorithms*, by A. V. Aho, J. E. Hopcroft, and J. D. Ullman, Addison Wesley, 1974; and are summarized in *Data Networks: Concepts, Theory and Practice*, by Uyless Black, Prentice Hall, 1989.

This figure shows an example of how algorithm A is applied, using node A as the source and node J as the destination (sink). (Please be aware that the topology represented in the figure was prepared for illustrative [not implementation] purposes.) Algorithm A is defined generally as:

- Least-cost criteria weights are assigned to the paths in the network.
- Each node is labeled (identified) with its least-cost criteria from the source along a known path. Initially, no paths are known, so each node is labeled with infinity. However, updates to the values (once the weights are established) are the same as an initialization.
- Each node is examined in relation to all nodes adjacent to it. (The source node is the first node considered and becomes the working node.) This step is actually a one-time occurrence, wherein the source node is initialized with the costs of all its adjacent nodes.
- Least-cost criteria labels are assigned to each of the nodes adjacent to the working node. Labels change if a shorter path is found from this node to the source node.
- The link-state database is used to build the shortest-path tree.
- And the process proceeds as explained in the next section.

Application of Algorithm A

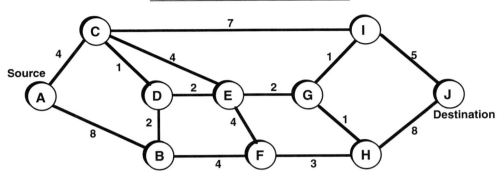

A Becomes the Working Node

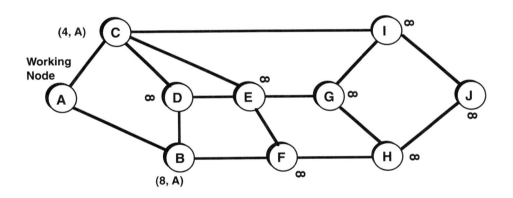

Notes:

_____

_____

_____

_____

After the adjacent nodes are labeled (or relabeled), all other nodes in the network are examined. If one has a smaller value in its label, its label becomes permanent, and it becomes the working node.

If the sum of the node's label is less than the label on an adjacent node, the adjacent node's label is changed, because a shorter path has been found to the source node. In the top figure, node E is relabeled because node D is a shorter route through node C.

The selection of node D as the working node reveals that node A has a better path to node B than the path calculated in previous step. The path from A through C, D, and D is 7. The previous path was a direct connection from A to B. One might wonder how the path through multiple nodes is better than a direct connection. It can occur. For example, the link between A and B might be a low-speed, point-to-point link connecting these nodes across a campus. The links (or networks) between A, C, D, and B might be high-speed LANs. If the metric represents link speed, it is easy to see why the path with more links is preferable.

Another working node is selected and the process repeats itself until all possibilities have been searched. The final labels reveal the least-cost, end-to-end path between the source and the other nodes. These nodes are considered to be within a set N as it pertains to the source node.

C Becomes the Working Node

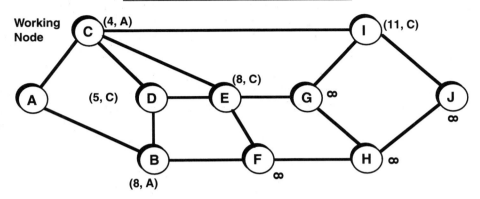

D Becomes the Working Node

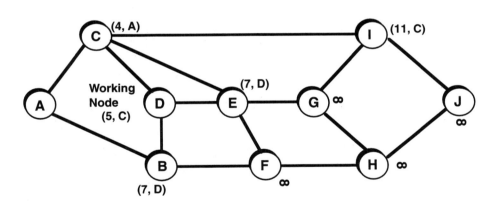

Notes:

_____

_____

_____

_____

The routing topology is shown in this figure. The numbers in parentheses represent the order of selection as reflected in the previous table.

Notice that the operation has created a spanning tree topology: (a) all nodes are connected to each other, and (b) there are no loops in the topology.

Of course, the links that have been blocked (pruned) are still present. They may be placed back into operation if necessary. For example, if an operational interface fails, the advertising messages will allow the routers or bridges in the routing domain to reconfigure their routing tables, and place the appropriate blocked link(s) back into operation.

Routing Topology for Node A

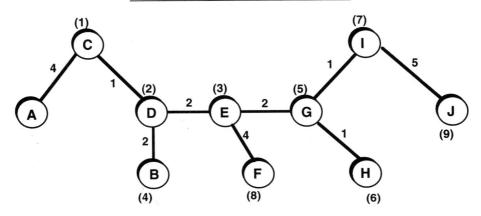

Notes:

_____

_____

_____

_____

_____

_____

Notes:

_____

_____

_____

_____

_____

_____

Summary

- Link state protocols look for a route between sender and receiver:

- ... with the "shortest path" between them

- Most use spanning tree operations

Lecture 6

LAN Bridges

Major Topics

- Placement of MAC bridge operations

- Types of bridges

- Packet filtering

- Learning about MAC addresses

Bridges are designed to interconnect LANs; therefore, it is convenient for them to use a MAC address in determining how to relay the traffic between LANs. Additionally, a bridge "pushes" the conventional network layer responsibilities of route discovery and relaying operations into the data link layer. In effect, a bridge has no conventional network layer. Bridges may also implement the SPF, which was just discussed.

This example shows a multiport bridge, which accepts a frame coming in on a port from network A. The frame is examined by the MAC relay entity, and a decision is made to relay the traffic on an output port to network C.

By virtue of the design of a bridge (no technical reason exists why a bridge could not exhibit more functionality), it has relatively limited buffering capability. Also, there is no provision for data integrity in bridges (such as the acknowledgment of traffic, and the possible retransmission of erred traffic). As a consequence, frames can be discarded if the bridge becomes congested. On the other hand, bridges are fast, and they are very easy to implement. Indeed, most bridges are self-configuring. This feature relieves network managers of many onerous tasks, such as constant management of a number of naming and network reconfiguration parameters.

Bridge Operations

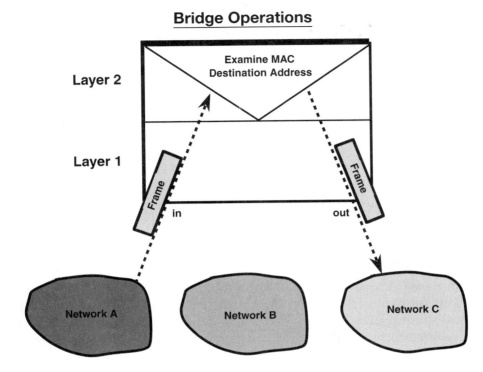

Where:
  MAC   Media access control (a LAN address)

Notes:

_____

_____

_____

_____

_____

_____

Several different kinds of bridges are available for internetworking LANs. The simplest and most basic type of bridge is called the *transparent bridge* (also known by some people as a "no frills" bridge). This bridge simply receives traffic coming in on each port and stores the traffic until it can be transmitted on the outgoing ports. It will not forward the traffic from the port from which it was received. The bridge does not make any conversion of the traffic. It does not slow down the internetwork LANs. It merely extends LANs beyond what could be achieved with simple repeaters. The basic bridge will allow LANs attached to it to transmit at the same time and it will not allow these transmissions to incur collisions. However, it should be noted that internetworking of multiple networks through the simple bridges does not increase the capacity since these simple operations relay traffic from one LAN to every other LAN on the network. The combined transmission rates cannot exceed the basic rate of each LAN. There are certain exceptions to this statement, because a bridge might accept traffic for a short period of time beyond the peak rate through the use of buffering capabilities.

The source routing bridge is so named because the route is determined by the source of the traffic. In addition, the routing header, contained in the protocol data unit, contains information on the route that the traffic takes through the Internet.

A transparent learning bridge "finds out" where the location of stations are by examining source and destination addresses in the frame when it is received at the bridge. The destination address is stored if it is not in routing cache and sent to all LANs except the LAN from which it came. In turn, the source address is stored and the direction from which it came as well. Consequently, if another frame is received in which this source address is now a destination address, it is forwarded across this port. The only restriction to the use of a transparent learning bridge is that the physical topology cannot allow loops.

The last type of bridge is called a *spanning tree* (or *transparent spanning*) bridge. Unlike the previous examples in this explanation, the spanning tree bridge uses a subnet of the full topology to create a loop-free operation.

Types of Bridges

Transparent basic bridge:
  Places incoming frame onto all outgoing
  ports except original incoming port

Source routing bridge:
  Relies on routing information in frame
  to relay to an outgoing port

Transparent learning bridge
  Stores the origin of a frame (from which port)
  and later uses to relay frames to that port

Transparent spanning bridge
  Uses a subset of the LAN topology
  to create a loop-free operation

Notes:

_____

_____

_____

_____

_____

_____

This figure provides examples of how a bridge forwards and filters frames. A frame transmitted on the LAN from A to B is not forwarded by bridge 1. The bridge assumes the traffic was successfully transferred on the broadcast network between A and B. This concept is called *filtering*.

Traffic destined from station A to station C must be forwarded by bridge 1 in order to reach station C. However, this frame is discarded (filtered) by bridge 2.

Both bridges 1 and 2 must forward traffic destined from station A to station D.

Discarding Frames at the Bridges

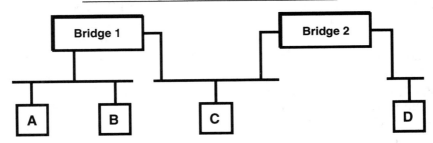

A ——▶ B =   Discard by Bridge 1

A ——▶ C =   Forward from Bridge 1; Discard by Bridge 2

A ——▶ D =   Both Bridges Forward

Notes:

_____

_____

_____

_____

_____

This figure shows a decision flowchart used by a spanning tree bridge to (a) determine the destination port for a frame and (b) update the routing database. Upon receiving a frame from a port (in this example, port A), the bridge examines the routing directory to determine if the destination MAC address exists. If not, the frame is broadcast to all ports except the source port (port A). If the address exists in the database, it is forwarded to the appropriate port. Otherwise, the frame is discarded.

The next step is to determine if the MAC source address that was in the frame exists in the routing database. If it does not exist, the address is added to the database with an entry revealing that it came from port A. A timer is set on this entry in order to keep the routing database up-to-date. If the database becomes full, older entries are cashed out. If the source address already exists in the database, the direction is checked, perhaps refreshed, and the timer is reset.

Learning Bridge Logic

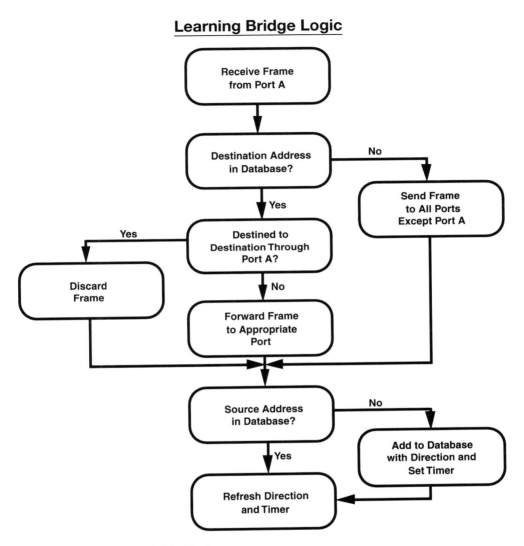

From: IEEE Network, Vol 2, No 1.

Notes:

_____

_____

_____

A source routing network requires that the routing information be furnished in the protocol data unit (PDU) that is transmitted across the network. Typically, this routing information is embedded into a header shown in this figure as "routing information."

At a minimum, routing information must identify the intermediate nodes that are required to receive and send the PDU. While vendor's implementations vary, in implementing source routing a general practice is to provide the LAN and bridge that is to receive and send the PDU.

Therefore, source routing requires that the user traffic follow a path that is determined by the routing information field.

One can reasonably ask, "Is source routing effective vis-à-vis the inherent overhead incurred?" The answer to this question is that source routing does provide a means to develop optimum routes, but it also entails a considerable amount of overhead.

Source Routing Concept

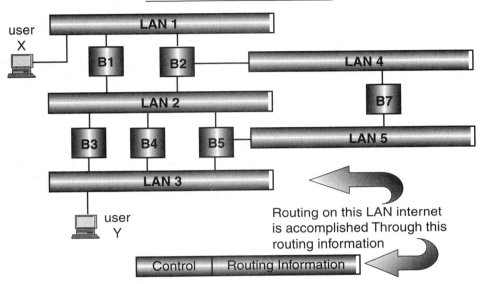

Routing on this LAN internet is accomplished Through this routing information

Control	Routing Information

Notes:

_____

_____

_____

_____

_____

_____

In many situations, it is not possible for LANs to interwork directly with bridges between LANs. Since many enterprises are widely distributed, the LANs must often be connected with wide area communications links. These links connect LAN bridges as a point-to-point topology. Such a connection is called *remote bridging.* Some vendors, such as AppleTalk, refer to the bridges as *half bridges* in the sense that two bridges and the link are considered to be a single bridge.

Spanning tree operations can be applied to remote bridges. The point-to-point link is considered to be part of the spanning tree, and the bridges are obligated to forward traffic on that link to the other bridge.

That is the good news. The bad news is that the IEEE, in its initial discussions on spanning tree bridges, did not fully define remote bridge operations. Therefore, vendors have taken it upon themselves to define procedures for two remote bridges to communicate with each other and determine if traffic is to be forwarded through the point-to-point link.

Another issue that should be considered is the fact that if a LAN is connected through bridges into wide area network (WAN) topologies, with rare exceptions, these WANs will not provide the broadcasting capability. Therefore, it may be necessary for disbursed LANs to have their bridges fully meshed in order for the bridges to communicate with each other. This fully meshed network, while expensive, allows each designated LAN bridge to communicate with the other dedicated LAN bridges.

As of this writing, the 802 committee is addressing the issue of adapting standardized procedures for remote bridge operations. Decisions being contemplated include:

- How one bridge on the point-to-point link decides or does not decide how to forward traffic
- How the traffic is represented from the standpoint of its syntax on the point-to-point link
- How bridges can communicate with other bridges using not only the point-to-point link method, but a wide area switched network as well

Remote Bridges

(Also called half bridges)

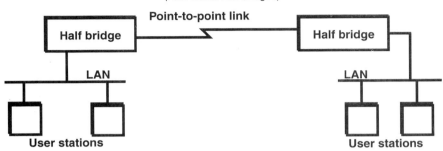

Notes:

_____

_____

_____

_____

_____

_____

Notes:

_____

_____

_____

_____

_____

_____

Summary

Bridges:

- Operate at L_2 of the Model

- Use MAC addresses for forwarding traffic

- Come in several varieties

- Connect LANs together

Notes:

_____

_____

_____

_____

_____

_____

Lecture 7

IP Routing Protocols in Action

Major Topics

- Route discovery between routing domains

- Using a backup route

- Example of a route advertisement message

This figure shows internetworking concepts in more detail. This example is generic in that it does not illustrate any specific protocol. It uses concepts taken from several protocols.

For simplicity, the networks between the routers are not included in this figure. In this manner, the only two machines that need know about both autonomous systems are C and X.

Routers C and X are designated as core routers for autonomous systems 1 and 2, respectively. The same concepts apply to areas, but this section will use the term *autonomous systems*. In this figure, router C's routing information (shown on the left side of the figure) is sent to router X, which uses it to update its routing table containing reachability information pertaining to nodes A, B, C, D, E, F, and G. Router X is not concerned with how this information was obtained by router C. It could have been obtained by an IGP method, but these internal operations remain transparent to router X.

Routing Domains

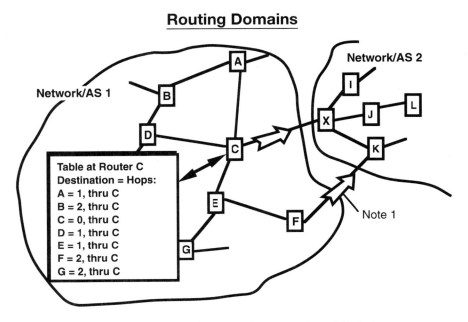

Note 1: Multiple routers may advertise out of a network or AS, but
         practice is for a network to establish one designated
         router to advertise on behalf of the network. For an AS,
         multiple AS border routers may advertise.

Notes:

_____

_____

_____

_____

_____

_____

To expand this discussion, let us assume routers F and K also exchange routing information. An autonomous system is not restricted to only one core router, but an area may designate only one router for the area. Now assume that the link or network connection is lost between E and F. router C discovers this problem through its IGP and typically enters a value denoting infinity (Inf) in its routing table entry to F (16, 256, or whatever the protocol stipulates).

An "F=Inf, through C" message is sent to router X as shown by the arrow from C to X.

Effect of Losing a Network Connection

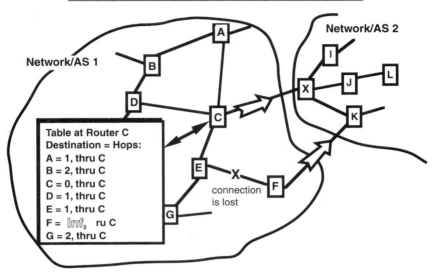

Notes:

_____

_____

_____

_____

_____

_____

However, router X likely knows of a better route. Since F and K have exchanged routing information, the IGP exchange between X and K reveals that a better path than 16 exists to F. X stores in its routing table that this path is through K. It also sends an EGP message to core router C that F can be reached through X with a cost metric of 3. Since 3 is less than 16, router C updates its routing table accordingly.

Receiving Routing Information from Router X

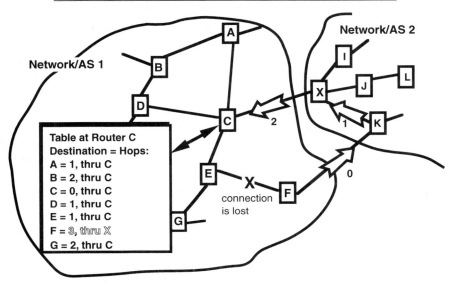

Table at Router C
Destination = Hops:
A = 1, thru C
B = 2, thru C
C = 0, thru C
D = 1, thru C
E = 1, thru C
F = 3, thru X
G = 2, thru C

Note: Be aware that this operation is not permitted in some systems

Notes:

This figure shows an example of an update message in relation to the Internet topology examples discussed in previous discussions.

In this figure, the networks between the routers have been labeled with arbitrary network IDs. Router C issues the update message in this figure to router X. The message contains a header to identify the sending node and perhaps other fields, such as sequence numbers, time stamps, and authentication parameters. One field in the header specifies how many distances are being reported in the message; in this example, the value is 3.

The data field is of interest to us here. Three distance groups are reported in the data field: 0 = networks directly attached to C (D1); 1 = networks one hop away from C (D2); and 2 = networks two hops away from C (D3).

Four addresses are being reported at D1: 14.4, 128.5, 128.3, and 128.2. Six addresses are being reported at D2: 15.7, 128.11, 14.2, 128.1, 13.1, and 13.2. Four addresses are being reported at D3: 15.1, 128.9, 13.9, and 14.1.

Once again, this example is general and generic, and in later parts of this course, we will look at the messages of the specific routing protocols, such as RIP and OSPF.

An Update Message (Generic)

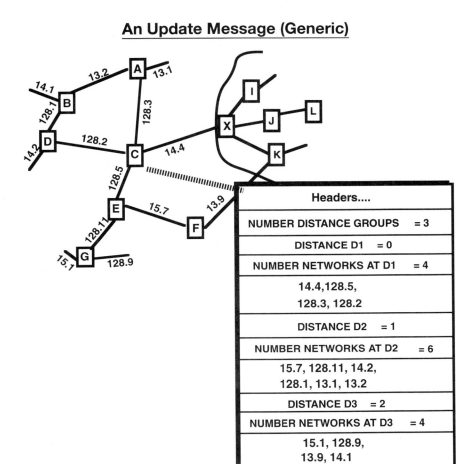

Headers....		
NUMBER DISTANCE GROUPS		= 3
DISTANCE D1	= 0	
NUMBER NETWORKS AT D1		= 4
14.4,128.5, 128.3, 128.2		
DISTANCE D2	= 1	
NUMBER NETWORKS AT D2		= 6
15.7, 128.11, 14.2, 128.1, 13.1, 13.2		
DISTANCE D3	= 2	
NUMBER NETWORKS AT D3		= 4
15.1, 128.9, 13.9, 14.1		

Notes:

_____

_____

_____

_____

_____

Notes:

_____

_____

_____

_____

_____

_____

Summary

- Routing domains often provide backup for each other

- Backup is through alternate routes

- Route advertisements provide information on possible alternate paths

Lecture 8

Network Address Translation (NAT)

Major Topics

- Private IP Addresses

- Overloading IP addresses

- Virtual addresses

There are instances when an organization has no need to connect into the Internet or another private intranet. Therefore, it is not necessary to adhere to the IP addressing registration conventions, and the organization can use the addresses it chooses. It is important that it is certain that connections to other networks will not occur, since the use of addresses that are allocated elsewhere could create problems.

In RFC 1597, several IP addresses have been allocated for private addresses, and it is a good idea to use these addresses if an organization chooses not to register with the Internet. Systems are available that will translate private, unregistered addresses to public, registered addresses if connections to global systems are needed.

Private IP Addresses

- The addresses set aside for private allocations:

    Class A addresses: 10.x.x.x - 10.x.x.x (1)

    Class B addresses: 172.16.x.x - 172.31.x.x (16)

    Class C addresses: 192.168.0.x - 192.168.255.x (256)

Notes:

_____

_____

_____

_____

_____

_____

The Network Address Translation (NAT) allows an organization to use private, non-registered IP addresses (non-globally routable addresses) within its own routing domain. If traffic is to be sent out of this domain, NAT translates these addresses to globally routable addresses. The reverse process occurs at the router for traffic received by the domain. NAT thus allows an organization to use its own private addresses. It also supports a process called the TCP load distribution feature that allows the mapping of a single global address to multiple non-global addresses. This feature is used to conserve addresses, and is explained shortly. NAT is described in RFC 1631, and examples used in this discussion are sourced from this RFC and [CISC98].[1]

This figure is used to introduce the basic concepts of NAT. First, a couple of definitions are in order. An *inside local IP address* is a non-global address that is assigned to a host. This host resides on an inside network—one that uses non-global addresses. An *inside global IP address* is a global address and represents the inside address to the outside networks (global addressing networks). Router A in this figure houses a NAT table that correlates these addresses.

The bottom part of the figure shows how NAT is used to map addresses between the inside and outside networks. In event 1, host B sends an IP datagram to host D, through router A. Router A checks the address in the datagram and knows that source address (SA) 172.16.1.1 is an inside address. If an entry in the NAT table does not exist, the router dynamically selects an available global address from a pool of addresses and creates an entry in the table. In event 2, the router replaces the inside SA with the corresponding outside SA, and forwards the datagram.

In event 3, host D replies and uses its SA of 191.1.1.3 and the NAT global address for the destination address (DA) of 191.1.1.1. This datagram is received by router A, which performs the mapping of the global DA of 191.1.1.1 to the inside DA of 172.16.1.1, depicted as event 4 in the figure.

NAT is a straightforward configuration; essentially the local IP and global IP addresses are entered into the table during the configuration, along with the inside and outside interfaces on the router.

---

[1]Cisco IOS Switching Services, Cisco Press, 1998.

Network Address Translation (NAT)

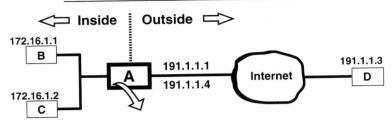

NAT Table

Inside local IP address	Inside global IP address
172.16.1.1	191.1.1.1
172.16.1.2	191.1.1.4

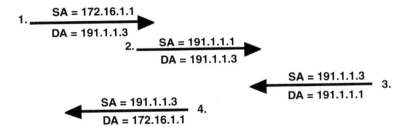

Where:
   DA   Destination IP address
   DP   Destination port number
   SA   Source IP address
   SP   Source port number

Notes:

_____

_____

_____

_____

_____

NAT allows the reuse of inside global addresses by mapping one of these addresses to more than one local address. This operation is called *overloading an inside global address*. The ability to maintain unambiguous identification of all user sessions is through the inside local address, the inside global address, plus the port numbers that are carried in the TCP or UDP segment header.

NAT defines another address; it is called the *outside global IP address*, and it is a conventional IP address assigned to a host on the globally addressable outside network.

This figure shows how this part of NAT works. In event 1, host B sends a datagram to host D, through router A. The figure shows the source address (SA), source port (SP), destination address (DA), and destination port (DP). The router intercepts the datagram, and performs either static or dynamic translation of the inside local IP address (172.16.1.1) to a shared inside global IP address (191.1.1.1).

In event 2, the router forwards the datagram toward the destination host D. In event 3, host D replies. The host simply exchanges the destination address and port number with the source address and port number.

Router A receives this datagram and looks at the NAT table to determine what it is to do. It uses the socket pair shown in event 3 as a key to the table.

In event 4, the translation is made back to host B's inside local IP address, and the datagram is delivered to host B in the inside network. The same operation can be performed for host C, using the second entry in the NAT table.

The configuration at the router entails the allocation of a pool of global addresses as needed, and the correlation of them with the inside addresses and the associated input and output interfaces.

Overloading Inside Global Addresses

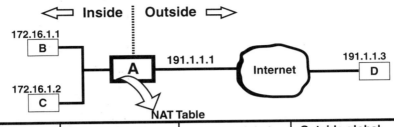

Protocol	Inside local IP address: port nr.	Inside global IP address: port nr.	Outside global IP address: port nr.
TCP	172.16.1.1:1500	191.1.1.1:1500	191.1.1.3:25
TCP	172.16.1.2:3001	191.1.1.1:3001	191.1.1.3:25

```
         SA = 172.16.1.1
1.       SP = 1500          ─────►
         DA = 191.1.1.3
         DP = 25

              SA = 191.1.1.1
2.            SP = 1500          ─────►
              DA = 191.1.1.3
              DP = 25

                   SA = 191.1.1.3
                   SP = 25          3.
              ◄─── DA = 191.1.1.1
                   DP = 1500

         SA = 191.1.1.3
         SP = 25          4.
    ◄─── DA = 172.16.1.1
         DP = 1500
```

Where:
DA   Destination IP address
DP   Destination port number
SA   Source IP address
SP   Source port number

Notes:

_____

_____

NAT has several other useful features, and one of them merits a description here. It has nothing to do with IP address management, but it is concerned with the distribution of workload across multiple hosts. The operation can be useful in a situation where a host is overloaded with work. For example, a name server may be heavily used, and it is a relatively simple matter to download a Domain Name System (DNS) file from the authoritative name server to one or more hosts and to use them to absorb the extra work. This figure shows how NAT is used to support *TCP load distribution.*

The key to this operation is to configure the router with the IP addresses of the hosts that will share the workload (they are called *real hosts*) and to indicate that these hosts belong to a rotary pool. Another IP address is set up to identify a *virtual host.* This "host" does not exist, and its address is used by the router to identify the rotary group; it is shown as host V in this figure. Once the system is configured, the operations are similar to the examples covered earlier.

When the NAT gateway receives the IP datagram in event 3, it does a NAT table lookup using the inside local address and port number, and the outside address and port number as the key. Therefore, if, say, host D sends another TCP session to node A, it must have a different port number than 1500 (say 1501) in its source port field (an ongoing rule is that duplicate source port numbers cannot emanate from the same host). However, multiple entries in the NAT table for node D are still unique, because even though the address (191.1.1.3) is the same for these entries, the two port numbers are different (1500, 1501). If node E sends the same source port number 1500 or 1501, its address is different, so the NAT table entries are still unique.

TCP Load Distribution

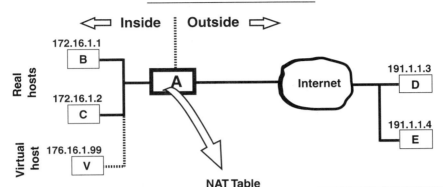

⇐ **Inside** ┊ **Outside** ⇒

Real hosts

172.16.1.1
B

172.16.1.2
C

A

Internet

191.1.1.3
D

191.1.1.4
E

Virtual host

176.16.1.99
V

NAT Table

Protocol	Inside local IP address: port nr.	Virtual Host IP address: port nr.	Outside global IP address: port nr.
TCP	172.16.1.1:53	176.16.1.99:53	191.1.1.3:1500
TCP	172.16.1.2:53	176.16.1.99:53	191.1.1.3:1501

1.
SA = 191.1.1.3
SP = 1501
DA = 176.16.1.99
DP = 53

2.
SA = 191.1.1.3
SP = 1500
DA = 172.16.1.1
DP = 53

3.
SA = 172.16.1.1
SP = 53
DA = 191.1.1.3
DP = 1500

4.
SA = 176.16.1.99
SP = 53
DA = 191.1.1.3
DP = 1500

Notes:

Notes:

_____

_____

_____

_____

_____

_____

Summary

- NAT allows the reuse of IP addresses

- NAT has helped relieve the burden on the
  IP address space

- NAT is used in many internetworking operations

Lecture 9

Major Attributes
of the Protocols

Major Topics

- A taxonomy of routing protocols

- Overview of protocols in relation to taxonomy

- Protocol comparisons

Notes:

_____

_____

_____

_____

_____

_____

Major Attributes of Routing Protocols

- Type: Type of path created:
  D-V: Distance-vector
  L-S: Link-state

- Path: Path advertising values

- I or E: IGP or EGP

- Over: Runs over which protocol

- Neigh: Neighbor discovery capabilities

- Sec: Security is part of the protocol

- Change: How changes are handled
  D: Dynamic; P: Partial table; F: Full table

- Agg: Address aggregation

- Asymm: Asymmetrical routing on a link

Notes:

_____

_____

_____

_____

_____

Public and private internets have implemented a number of route advertising protocols, some of which have become international standards. An
earlier implementation of a routing protocol is the gateway-to-gateway
protocol (GGP). This protocol is a distance-vector protocol and was originally designed to be used in the ARPAnet backbone. It is not used today
due to its overhead and restriction in operating only on core backbones.

The External Gateway Protocol (EGP) is also a distance-vector protocol and was the prevalent standard for use between networks. It over-
came some of the problems of EGP, but is also not used much today.

The Routing Information Protocol (RIP) is a distance-vector protocol,
which was designed by Xerox's Palo Alto Research Laboratories (PARC)
for use on LANs, although it is used today in many WANs. RIP had some
design flaws when it was introduced into the industry. Several have been
corrected by RFCs and/or vendor-specific solutions.

The Open Shortest Path First (OSPF) protocol is a link state protocol and has been designed to solve some of the problems found in RIP and
other internal gateway protocols. OSPF is relatively new to the industry
but its use is growing rapidly.

The Border Gateway Protocol (BGP) is designed to perform route
discovery between autonomous systems. It overcomes some of the problems of EGP. BGP is a prevalent protocol in the Internet and is used between autonomous systems and ISPs.

Finally, the Interdomain Routing Protocol (IDRP) is an OSI protocol. It is not used much in North America.

A newcomer to the industry is the private network-to-network interface (PNNI). It is based on using ATM in the network(s), and provides
two major functions: (a) route advertising and network topology analysis,
and (b) connection management (setting up and tearing ATM connections).

Cisco implements a proprietary routing protocol called the Inter-
Gateway Routing Protocol (IGRP). It is similar to RIP except it uses several metrics instead of hop count and a change result in the full table
being exchanged.

Routing Protocols

<u>Routing Information Protocol (RIP)</u>
   A distance vector protocol
   Intended for use on broadcast LANs
   Widely used today, with several variations

<u>Open Shortest Path First (OSPF)</u>
   A link state protocol
   Designed to overcome limitations of RIP
   Widely used today

<u>Intermediate System-to-Intermediate System (IS-IS)</u>
   A link state protocol
   Designed by Digital, similar to OSPF

<u>Border Gateway Protocol (BGP)</u>
   Overcomes some limitations of EGP
   Preferred protocol between ASs

<u>Interdomain Routing Protocol (IDRP)</u>
   An OSI-based protocol

<u>Private Network-to-Network Interface (PNNI)</u>
   A newcomer
   Based on using an ATM network

<u>Inter-Gateway Routing Protocol (IGRP)</u>
   Cisco's "RIP" with metric advertising

Notes:

_____

_____

_____

This table provides a summary and comparison of several of the key routing protocols. Using the legend below the table, the table is self-descriptive.

The lecturer will take you through the Routing Protocol Comparison Chart to provide some additional thoughts.

Routing Protocol Comparison Chart

Protocol	Type	Path	I or E	Over	Neigh	Sec	Change	Agg	Asymm
RIP	D-V	Hop	IGP	UDP	No	Yes	D/F	Yes	No
OSPF	L-S	Metric	IGP	IP	Yes	Yes	D/P	Yes	Yes
BGP	D-V/ L-S	Policy	EGP	TCP	Yes	Yes	D/P	Yes	Yes
IGRP	L-S	Metric	IGP	IP	No	Yes	D/P	Yes	No
EIGRP	L-S	Metric	IGP	IP	Yes	Yes	D/P	Yes	No
PNNI	L-S	Metric	IGP/ EGP	ATM	Yes	No	D/P	Yes	Yes

Legend:
- Type — Type of path created:
  - D-V: Distance-vector
  - L-S: Link-state
- Path — Path advertising values
- I or E — IGP or EGP
- Over — Runs over which protocol
- Neigh — Neighbor discovery capabilities
- Sec — Security part of the protocol
- Change — Changes handled:
  - D: Dynamic
  - P: Partial advertising
  - F: Full table advertising
- Agg — Address aggregation
- Asymm — Asymmetrical routing on a link

Notes:

_____

_____

_____

Notes:

_____

_____

_____

_____

_____

_____

Summary

- Major distinctions of routing protocols determine their functions and capabilities

- Older protocols use some form of minimum hop

- Newer protocols use link metrics, but often consider fewest hops as their approach

Lecture 10

RIP Basics

Major Topics

- How RIP advertises addresses

- Example of RIP routing updates

- The RIP messages

The Routing Information Protocol (RIP) system was developed based on research at the Xerox Palo Alto Research Center (PARC) and Xerox's PUP and XNS routing protocols. Interestingly, its wide use was attributed to the implementation at the University of California at Berkeley (UCB) in a number of LANs. UCB also distributed RIP with its UNIX system. It is rather ironic that RIP is designed for LANs, yet is now used in some wide area networks—if for no other reason than the fact that it's there. That is, it was distributed as part of the Internet suite of protocols, and was one of the first simple routing protocols that gained wide use in private internets.

RIP is classified as a vector-distance algorithm routing protocol. RIP routing decisions are based on the number of intermediate "hops" to the final destination. Early descriptions of this type of protocol were described by L. R. Ford and D. R. Fulkerson (*Flows in Networks*, Princeton University Press, Princeton, NJ, 1962). Therefore, RIP is sometimes called a Ford-Fulkerson algorithm, or a Bellman-Ford algorithm, because R. E. Bellman devised the routing equation (*Dynamic Programming*, Princeton University Press, Princeton, NJ, 1957).

RIP advertises only network addresses and distances (number of hops). It uses a hop count to compute the route cost, but it uses a maximum value of 16 to indicate that an address is unreachable.

The Routing Information Protocol (RIP)

- A distance vector protocol

- An IGP

- Designed for use on broadcast LANs

- Not intended for large networks

- Simple and robust

Notes:

_____

_____

_____

_____

_____

_____

This figure shows the general scheme for a RIP routing update. Router A advertises the address 172.16.0.0 to routers B and C. This updates occur during time period 1. (The notation 1a means the event occurs at about the same time as event 1, and the same idea is conveyed with 2a, 2b, and 2c.) Since A is directly attached to 176.16.0.0, it advertises a metric (hop count) of 1 to this address.

Routers B and C receive this advertisement and compare the address and the metric with their routing tables. Assuming A had previously notified B and C about 176.16.0.0, the routing table entries for this address would be a metric of 2, with the next node identified as router A. Routers A and B add 1 to the metric value in the RIP message and compare this value with their table entry. In this example, the two values are two, so the advertisement reveals no better path, and no new routes are found.

In time periods 2 and 2a, routers B and C advertise 176.16.0.0 to each other, after incrementing the metric in the message to 3. Since their routing table entries show a metric of 2, they ignore this message because it does not show a better route to 176.16.0.0.

In time periods 2b and 2c, routers B and C also advertise a metric of 2 to router A. Router A ignores these updates because its routing table has stored a better route to 172.16.0.0.

RIP Routing Updates

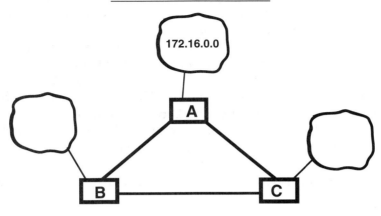

<u>**Updates:**</u>

1. A to B: 172.16.0.0 = 1

1a. A to C: 172.16.0.0 = 1

2.   B to C: 172.16.0.0 = 2

2a. C to B: 172.16.0.0 = 2

2b. B to A: 172.16.0.0 = 2

2c. C to A: 172.16.0.0 = 2

Notes:

_____

_____

_____

_____

_____

_____

Since all routers are receiving advertisements from each other, reachability can be computed to all networks. As an example, here is the routing table as viewed by router 3 (R3).

Destination is an address of the destination network, as seen by R3 (in TCP/IP-based networks, an IP address). Next hop (next node) is the address of the node that is to receive the traffic next. This entry is 0 in this table since there is no next hop. The Metric column states how many hops to the destination network. The Direct or Remote column is either D (directly attached) or R (a remote network, not directly attached). The Local or RIP column is either L (network discovered it because it is local) or R (network discovered it through RIP messages). The Interface column identifies the physical port on R5 on which the discovery was made.

RIP Routing Table Example

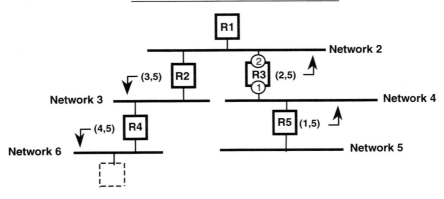

(n) = physical port (interface) number

RIP routing table at R3:

Destination	Next hop	Metric	Direct or Remote	Local or RIP	Interface
Network 2	0	1	D	L	2
Network 3	R2	2	R	R	2
Network 4	0	1	D	L	1
Network 5	R5	2	R	R	1
Network 6	R2	3	R	R	2

Notes:

_____

_____

_____

_____

_____

Since RIP updates its neighbors, and these neighbors update their neighbors, it takes time for the updates to propagate through the routing domain. A router that sends its entire routing table does so every 30 seconds. Therefore, the nodes at the "end" of the broadcast will not find out about the change until all intervening nodes have timed out and sent the information to their next node.

As each router receives the update from its neighbor, it checks the update fields for the IP address and its associated metric. If the metric (number of hops) for the address is better than the one for the same address in the routing table, the router updates its table by setting the next hop to the advertising neighbor, and adding one to the metric. That is, if the metric received in the message is 2, then the routing table entry is 3, which means, "If my neighbor is 2 hops away, I am 3." This router will then advertise the metric of 3 to its neighbors, and so on, until all routers in the domain know about the advertised address.

The routing table has an entry called *next node* (or *next hop*). When the message is received, RIP checks the sending address in the IP datagram against the next node entry in the table, and if they match, the metric in the message is checked against the metric in the table.

It is easy to see that RIP changes may take a long time to reach convergence. Later, we examine some changes made to RIP that improve upon this rather cumbersome operation.

Network 1 Added to Topology

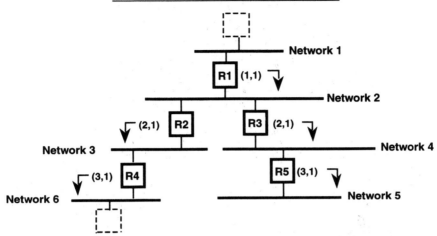

Convergence timing to learn about network 1:

Time	R1	R2	R3	R4	R5
1	1	–	–	–	–
2	1	2,R1	2,R1	–	–
3	1	2,R1	2,R1	3,R2	3,R3

Where: n,Rx means hop count, through Rx as the next node

Notes:

_____

_____

_____

_____

_____

RIP runs over UDP, so its messages are encapsulated into UDP segments, and it runs on a well-known port (number 520). There are two versions of RIP available: RIP-1 and RIP-2. This figure shows the message formats for both versions.

The command field can contain the values of 1 to 6, but 1 and 2 are the only formal (documented) values. A command code = 1 identifies a request message, and a value = 2 identifies a reply. The version field is 1 or 2 for the two versions.

The messages differ slightly. Both versions contain an address family, which is coded with a 2 for IP addresses. Next is an IP address and its metric (a hop count). These advertisement fields can be repeated 25 times. This limitation is to keep the RIP message less than 512 bytes (4 fixed bytes [command, version, 2 bytes of all zeroes] + 20 bytes × 25 repeats = 504 bytes).

For RIP-2, the unused fields in the RIP-1 message are coded as follows:

- Routing domain: Identifier of the routing daemon associated with this message. In UNIX, this field is a process ID. By the use of the routing domain, a machine can run multiple, concurrent RIPs.

- Route tag: If RIP is used to support exterior gateway protocols (EGPs), this field contains an autonomous system number.

- Subnet mask: Associated with the IP address in the message.

- Next hop IP address: If this field is 0, it indicates that datagrams should be sent to the address that is sending this RIP message. Otherwise, it contains an IP address, which indicates where the datagrams should be sent.

RIP Messages

0	7 8	15 16	31
Command	Version	All zeroes	
Address family		All zeroes	
IP address			
All zeroes			
All zeroes			
metric			
repeat of previous 20 bytes			

(a) RIP-1

0	7 8	15 16	31
Command	Version	Routing domain	
Address family		Route tag	
IP address			
Subnet mask			
Next hop IP address			
metric			
repeat of previous 20 bytes			

(b) RIP-2

Notes:

Notes:

_____

_____

_____

_____

_____

_____

Summary

- RIP is a simple distance metric protocol

- Revisions to the original release have corrected and improved RIP's operations

- RIP is widely-used in small routing domains

Lecture 11

RIP Operations

Major Topics

- Route advertising loops

- Improving convergence

RIP updates described so far are quite simple. However, this simplicity can cause some problems. One problem is the possibility of sending traffic through an inefficient path; the other is the possibility of a routing update taking a long time to reach convergence, during which the routing domain is unstable and not passing traffic efficiently and correctly.

To see why, we assume there is a failure on network 1 between host 1(H1) and router 1 (R1). In prior advertisements, R1 informed R2 and R3 that it was the node next to H1. Therefore, when R1 advertises infinity (16) metric to these routers, they should be able to know that they cannot reach H1. However, if either R1 or R2 send an update to R1 before they receive the bad news from this router, R1 will see that the advertised metric is 2 to H1. Let's concentrate on the operations between R1 and R2.

The way RIP is constructed, R1 does not know it is the only way to H1. Instead it updates its routing table, placing a metric of 3 into its table, and then, upon the next advertisement, sends a metric of 3 (to H1) to its neighbors. R1 now has its routing table "pointing" to R2 as the next node to H1.

The problem is indeed that R1 and R2 now point to each other as the node next to H1. Therefore, when R2 receives the message from R1 with a metric of 4 to H1, it must change its table to 5. Its next advertisement to R1 is a metric of 5 to H1. Since H1's table shows R2 as the node next to H1, it changes its table to 5, and its next advertisement to R2 is a 6.

The result is a loop, and the problem will continue until the metric reaches 16, at which time, the routers will reassess the situation and converge.

Counting to Infinity

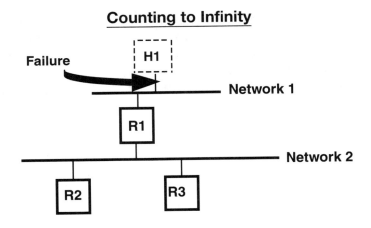

Upon failure, knowledge of route to H1:
   R1 knows: I = ~   R2 = 2   R3 = 2
   R2 knows: R1 = 1   R3 = 2
   R3 knows: R1 = 1   R2 = 2

Upon advertisement, choice of route to H1:
   R1: chooses R2 or R3 at a cost of   3
   R2: chooses R3 at a cost of   3   ⎫
   R3: chooses R2 at a cost of   3   ⎬ Loops!
                                               ⎭

Then R1 chooses R2 or R3 at a cost of   4...
....and so on......

Notes:

_____

_____

_____

_____

During the count to infinity operation, the advertisements are looping around between the routers in this example. As just mentioned, the looping continues until the maximum metric value of 16 is reached. At that time, H1 is indeed not reachable.

The process is quite inefficient. It leads to link congestion and the possibility of losing traffic, including RIP messages.

Loops During Convergence Ops

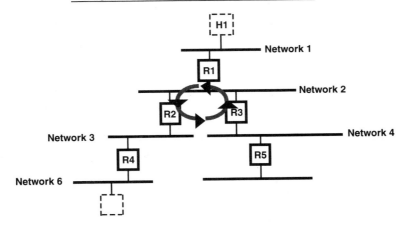

Until stabilization (convergence):

After 15 iterations: knowledge of route to H1:
   R1 knows: _
   R2 knows: _
   R3 knows: _
   ... as do other routers...

Notes:

_____

_____

_____

_____

_____

_____

Most RIP implementations have implemented measures to counteract the count to infinity problem. One change simply eliminates the 30-second timer; when a router has a routing update to send, it sends it immediately. Of course, this immediate update does not solve the problem, but it does speed up the time to reach convergence.

Another method is called *split horizon*. The idea behind this operation is based on the commonsense notion that it makes no sense for a router to advertise addresses through the interface from which it received the initial advertisement. In this figure, R1 would not receive advertisements from R2 or R3 about H1. That is, R1 and R2 cannot advertise H1 on their interface 1. This approach is effective in most situations, but it will not eliminate all problems. For example, if the physical network is a looped topology, the count to infinity problem still exists.

Steps to Improve Convergence

(a) Triggered Update:
    Don't wait 30 seconds
    When a change occurs, send update immediately

(b) Split Horizon:

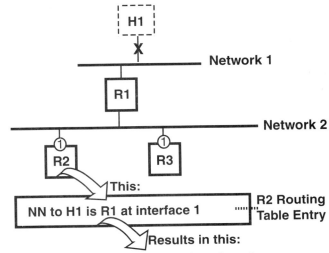

Therefore, don't advertise H1 on interface 1

Notes:

_____

_____

_____

_____

_____

_____

A variation to split horizon is *split horizon with poison reverse*. Instead of R2 and R3 not sending the H1 advertisements on their interface 1, they send the metric of 16. Of course, R1 ignores this information. If only two routers are involved, split horizon with poison reverse eliminates loops.

Another distance-vector protocol enhancement is called hold down. When a route is advertised as unreachable, the advertising router refuses to accept updates for a period of time after the route has been advertised. For example, after R1 sends the message to R2 and R3 with the infinity metric for H1, it will not accept advertisements for H1 from R2 or R3.

Hold down effectively constrains forwarding loops. It is not a cure-all and does increase the time to converge. RIP does not use hold down, but other distance-vector protocols do, such as Cisco's Inter-Gateway Routing Protocol (IGRP).

Steps to Improve Convergence
(Continued)

(c) Split Horizon with Poison Reverse:

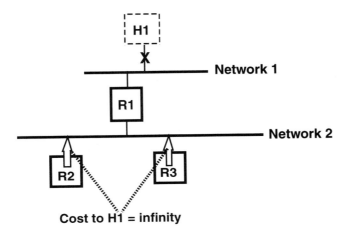

Cost to H1 = infinity

(d) Hold down:
Advertising router refuses updates from others
R1 refuses H1 updates from R2 and R3

Notes:

_____

_____

_____

_____

_____

Notes:

_____

_____

_____

_____

_____

_____

Summary

- Route advertising loops must be controlled within the routing domain

- RIP employs several operations to prevent loops and improve convergence

Lecture 12

MPLS and Label Distribution

Major Topics

- Multiprotocol Label Switching (MPLS)

- Label distribution and label binding

Label or tag switching is a topic of considerable interest in the Internet. The interest stems from the fact that traditional software-based routing is too slow to handle the large traffic loads in the Internet or an internet. Even with enhanced techniques, such as a fast-table lookup for certain datagrams, the load on the router is often more than the router can handle. The result may be lost traffic, lost connections, and overall poor performance in the IP-based network. Label or tag switching, in contrast to IP routing, is proving to be an effective solution to the problem.

Several methods are employed to implement label or tag switching. For this course, we examine those that are deployed, and under consideration. As we will see, many of them are similar variations on the same theme.

Some techniques use the concept of a flow, which is a sequence of user packets from one source machine or application to one or more machines or applications. For a "long" flow (many packets flowing between these entities), a router can cache information about the flow, and circumvent the traditional IP routing mechanisms (subnet masking, search on longest subnet mask, and so on) by storing the routing information in cache, thus achieving high throughput and low delay.

Label/Tag Switching

<u>Why?</u>

    Conventional IP routing is very slow

    Requires many operations (masking, best match)

    Enhance with high-speed label/tag switching

<u>What?</u>

    Correlate IP addresses, ports, etc. to simple label

    Use label as index to cache for routing information

Notes:

_____

_____

_____

_____

_____

The term functional equivalence class (FEC) is used throughout the industry and applied to new switching and routing operations. FEC is a general term and is used to describe an association of discrete packets with a destination address, usually the final recipient of the traffic, such as a host machine. Most FEC implementations also associate an FEC value with a destination address, and a class of traffic. The class of traffic is identified (typically) with a destination port number.

Why is FEC used? First, it allows the grouping of packets into classes. From this grouping, the FEC value in a packet can be used to set priorities for the handling of the packets, giving higher priority to certain FECs over others.

FECs can be used to support efficient QOS (quality of service) operations. For example, FECs can be associated with real-time voice traffic, low-priority newsgroup traffic, and so on.

The matching of the FEC with a packet is achieved by using a label to identify a specific FEC.

Another term has emerged in the past few months to describe FEC. It is called *layer 4 switching*. It means that part of the FEC is based on information contained in the layer 4 header. For the Internet protocols, the TCP/UDP port numbers make up these values. I prefer FEC to layer 4 switching. The latter term is not accurate, because the switching decisions are performed on more than port numbers.

Functional Equivalence Class (FEC)

<u>What?</u>

- An association of discrete packets with:

    A destination

    A class of traffic

<u>Why?</u>

- Allows the grouping of packets in FECs
- Allows the prioritization of FECs
- Supports efficient QOS operations

<u>Examples:</u>

- Destination addresses, Source addresses,

    Destination ports, Source ports

Notes:

_____

_____

_____

_____

_____

_____

One of the key aspects of high-speed forwarding systems is the use of a label or tag to identify the traffic. The assignment of the value to a packet varies, depending on the vendor's approach and/or the standard employed (an Internet RFC). This part of the course introduces the concepts of label allocation (binding), and in later discussions, we focus on more detailed examinations.

Parts of this discussion are sourced from the draft RFCs and white papers on Multiprotocol Label Switching (MPLS), and I thank the various authors for their contributions. I provide specific references on these sources later.

Local label allocation (local binding) refers to the operation in which the local node sets up a label relationship with an FEC. It can set this relationship up as it receives traffic, or it can set it up as it receives control information from an upstream or downstream neighbor. Remote binding is an operation in which a neighbor node assigns a binding to the local node. Typically, this is performed with control messages, such as a set up message.

Downstream label allocation refers to a method where the label allocation is done by the downstream LSR, i.e. the LSR that uses the label as an index into its switching tables. Proponents argue that this is the most natural label allocation/distribution mode for unicast traffic. As an LSR builds its routing tables (for control-driven allocation of tags) it is free, within some limits, to allocate labels in any manner that may be convenient to the particular implementation.

Upstream label allocation is done by the upstream LSR. In this case, the LSR choosing the label (the upstream LSR) and the LSR that needs to interpret packets using the label (the downstream LSR) are not the same node.

The broad category of control vs. data or flow-driven binding is distinguished by control binding being set up in advance with control messages or pre-provisioning craft commands to the node. Data or flow-control binding occurs dynamically, based on an analysis of the streaming packets.

Assignment and Binding Operations

<u>What?</u>
- Correlating an FEC with a label
- Informing neighbor nodes about labels

- Binding:

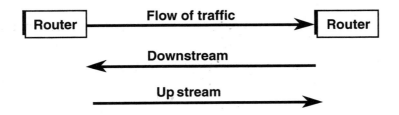

Notes:

_____

_____

_____

_____

_____

_____

This figure shows the entries in the LS tables for one path between users XYZ and HIJ. For this discussion, the path is identified with:

- Label 21: Identifies the path between user XYZ and switch A
  - a: is the output interface at XYZ
  - b: is the input interface at switch A
- Label 30: Identifies the path between switch A and switch B
  - d: is the output interface at switch A
  - a: is the input interface at switch B
- Label 21: Identifies the path between switch B and switch C
  - c: is the output interface at switch B
  - d: is the input interface at switch C
- Label 55: Identifies the path between switch C and user HIJ
  - a: is the output interface at switch C
  - b: is the input interface at HIJ

Several observations are noteworthy about this figure. First, there must be some means to associate the labels with the FEC and the addresses of the switches that participate in the operation. And the association must be made at each machine that participates in the end-to-end connection.

Second, in this example, the label is correlated with the sender's outgoing interface and the receiver's incoming interface. Since the labels are so-associated, they can be reused at each interface on the switches or user machines. In a sense, the interface numbers in the switch act as *internal* "tags" for the connection.

Example of Label Binding Operation

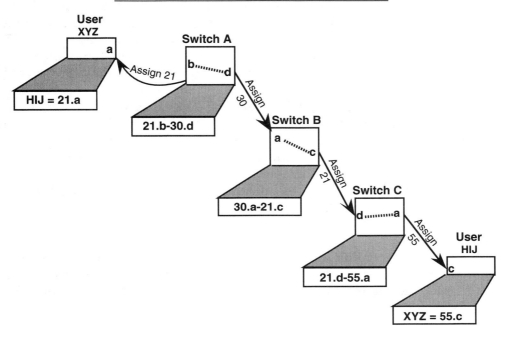

Notes:

_____

_____

_____

_____

_____

Third, the selection of the labels is a matter between the user and its adjacent switch, or between adjacent switches. Consequently, there is no requirement to keep the labels unambiguous across interfaces and through the network. For example, label 21 is used twice, between XYZ and switch A, and then between switches B and C. Trying to manage universal label values across multiple nodes and different networks would not be a very pleasant task.

Fourth, I show the label "bindings" (the association of the labels between nodes) in one direction only. It is a straightforward task to use the LS table in a bi-directional manner. For example, if the traffic were flowing from switch C to switch B, the LS table would appear as:

- Label 21:   Identifies the path between switch C and switch B
     d: is the output interface at switch C
     c: is the input interface at switch B

Fifth, this example does not show the next hop address, nor any QOS associated with the path. The next hop address is in the route columns in this figure and contains the IP address of the next hop. The QOS is subject to individual implementations.

Example of Label Binding Operations

(continued)

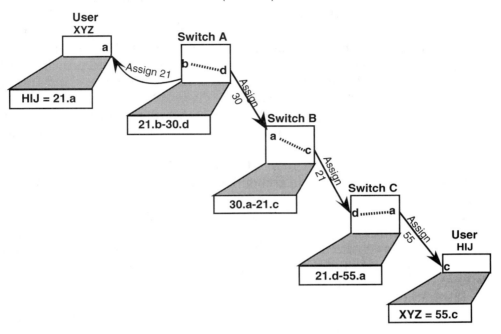

Notes:

_____

_____

_____

_____

_____

_____

Work is under way to develop the Multiprotocol Label Switching (MPLS) technology. As of this writing, it is not yet finished, and you may wish to obtain the Internet Draft document draft-ietf-mpls-framework-02.txt for more details. Be aware that the following discussion reflects the latest status of MPLS, but the final specification will reflect changes, although they will probably be minor. Our goal here is to focus on the principal aspects of MPLS, so I have summarized the major white papers and Internet Drafts, and provided tutorials and my views of the technology.

MPLS is a label swapping (mapping) forwarding technology, but it integrates label swapping with network layer routing. The idea is to improve the performance of network layer routing and the scalability of the network layer. An additional goal of the IETF Network Working Group is to provide greater flexibility in the delivery of routing services (by allowing new routing services to be added without a change to the forwarding paradigm). MPLS does not make a forwarding decision with each L_3 datagram, but an FEC is associated with a class of datagrams, and a fixed-length label is then negotiated between neighbor LSRs from the ingress to the egress of a routing domain.

The initial MPLS efforts of the Working Group are to focus on IPv4 and IPv6. Later, the core technology will be extendible to multiple network layer protocols, such as IPX, and SNA. The basic idea is not to restrict MPLS to any specific link layer technology.

In addition, MPLS does not require one specific label distribution protocol; it assumes there may be more than one, such as RSVP, BGP, or the Label Distribution Protocol (LDP).

Multiprotocol Label Switching (MPLS)

- Work underway in the IETF Network Working Group

- Goals:

  Standardize a label swapping technology

  Network layer independent

- Initial efforts directed to IPv4 and IPv6

- Does not dictate the specific label distribution
  protocol. Might be RSVP, BGP, or LDP

Notes:

_____

_____

_____

_____

_____

Notes:

_____

_____

_____

_____

_____

_____

Summary

- IP forwarding is being replaced in backbones

- Replacements involve some form of
  label switching

- Route discovery is still performed with
  IP addresses

Lecture 13

OSPF Basics

Major Topics

- Major functions of OSPF

- Directed graphs

- Link state advertisements (LSAs)

- Partitioning routing domains into areas

Open Shortest Path First (OSPF) is an IGP: Routers are all within one autonomous system. OSPF is a link state or shortest path first protocol, in contrast to some of the earlier Internet protocols which are based on some type of Bellman-Ford approach. The protocol, although relying on techniques designed outside of an internet environment, is tailored specifically for an internet and includes such capabilities as subnet addressing and type of service (TOS) routing.[1]

OSPF bases its routing discovery decisions on addresses and link state metrics. Once the decision is made on how to route the IP datagram, the datagram is routed without additional headers; that is to say, no additional encapsulation occurs.

OSPF is classified as a dynamic, adaptive protocol in that it adjusts to problems in the network (only a link or node failure) and provides short convergence periods to stabilize the routing tables. It is also designed to prevent looping of traffic, which is quite important in mesh networks or in LANs where multiple routers may be available to connect different LANs.

OSPF is encapsulated into the IP datagram data field. The IP protocol ID for OSPF is 89.

---

[1]TOS routing is not deployed in the Internet, although it was intended in the original specifications that it be an important aspect of OSPF. Check your installation for possible TOS support.

OSPF

- An area is a routing domain

- Dynamic, adapts to topology and metric changes

- Routers in area have identical link state database

- Database contains routers' local "state",
  usable interfaces and reachable neighbors

- Floods advertisements to all routers in area

- Each network has a designated router
  for the reduction of traffic flow

- Same algorithm for all routers: Spanning Tree

Notes:

_____

_____

_____

_____

_____

_____

OSPF works with the use of directed graphs. The graphs contain values between two points, either networks or routers. The values represent the weighted shortest path value with the router established as the root. Consequently, the shortest path tree from the router to any point in an internet is determined by the router performing the calculation. The calculation only reveals the next hop to the destination in the hop-to-hop forwarding process. The link state database used in the calculation is derived from the information obtained by advertisements by the routers to their neighbors, with periodic flooding throughout the autonomous system.

The information focuses on the topology of the network(s) with a directed graph. Routers and networks form the vertices of the graph. Periodically, this information can broadcast (flooded) to all routers in the autonomous system, or sent as needed, based on a change. An OSPF router computes the shortest path to the other routers in the routing domain based on the link state database.

Conceptually, separate cost metrics can be computed for each IP TOS. If the calculations reveal that two paths are of equal value, OSPF will distribute the traffic equally on these paths. In practice, the TOS idea has not been implemented in the Internet. Moreover, most implementations simply use the same value for each direction on the link.

Directed Graphs

Directed Graph

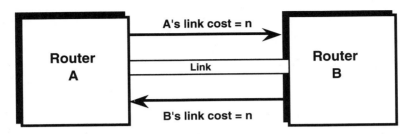

Separate metrics for One Link

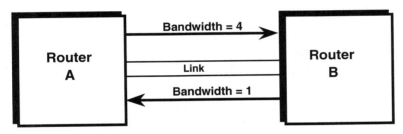

Notes:

_____

_____

_____

_____

_____

_____

OSPF's operations vary, depending upon the type of network in which it operates. Its behavior is slightly different if it is on a point-to-point network, a broadcast network, and multicast network and so on. For this discussion, we will examine the overall operations of OSPF that pertain to all network types.

OSPF implements a Hello protocol. It is a handshaking protocol that enables the routers to learn about each other, exchange information, and later perform pings with neighbor routers to make certain the link and/or router is up.

After the Hello operations have been completed, the peer routers are considered to be *merely adjacent*. This term means the routers have completed part of the synchronization, but not all of it.

Next, the routers exchange information that describes their knowledge of the routing domain. This information is called a database description and is placed in link state advertisement (LSA) messages. The database descriptions are not the entire link state database, but contain sufficient information for the receiving router to know if its link state database is consistent with its peer's databases. If all is consistent, the neighbor is now defined as *fully adjacent*. Otherwise, the routers then exchange LSAs containing link state updates, eventually becoming fully adjacent.

Thereafter, periodic Hellos are issued to keep peers aware of each other. Also, the LSAs that the router originated must be sent to its peers every 30 minutes, just to make certain all link state databases are the same.

OSPF is quite concerned with link state database synchronization, and most of the OSPF code is devoted to this very task.

Basic Operations of OSPF

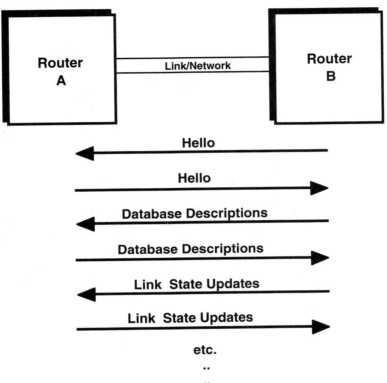

Notes:

_____

_____

_____

_____

_____

_____

Enterprises with large systems may operate with many networks, routers, and host computers. In order to manage this vast array of communications components, it is quite possible that many messages must be exchanged between the routers in order to determine how to relay traffic within the autonomous system between the sending computer and the receiving computer.

The network administrator must evaluate how much routing traffic is to be sent between the routers, because this routing traffic can affect the throughput of user data. A common practice in route advertising and route discovery is to flood the advertisements to all nodes in the routing domain. While measures can be taken to reduce the amount of duplicate traffic that a node receives, it is not unusual for networks to have their routing nodes connected in such as fashion to create loops, which means that it is possible for an advertisement to be received more than one time. Certainly, loops can be managed, and in most implementations, measures are taken to prevent loops for user traffic—but not for the route advertising traffic.

In simple terms, measures must be taken to keep this overhead traffic to a minimum, and we shall see that protocols such as OSPF implement a variety of rules to reduce unwarranted overhead.

A Larger Internet

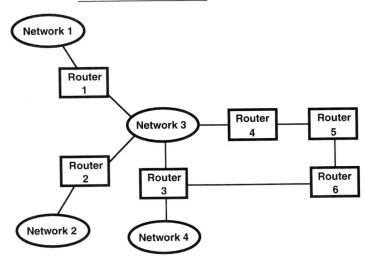

Potential Problems:
    Large routing tables
    Large routing messages
    Excessive routing traffic
    Resources needed to process traffic

Notes:

_____

_____

_____

_____

_____

We have learned that enterprises with large systems may operate with many networks, routers, and host computers. One effective solution that is used by OSPF is to divide or partition the autonomous system into smaller parts, called *areas*. This approach reduces the amount of router traffic that is sent through the autonomous system, because the areas are isolated from each other. This practice reduces the amount of information a router must maintain about the full autonomous system. Also, it means that the overhead information transmitted between routers to maintain OSPF routing tables is substantially reduced.

A designated router, say router 3 in this example, assumes the responsibility for informing the routers in the area about the other routers, networks, and host computers that exist in the entire autonomous system. As a consequence of this approach, the routers within the area are not concerned about the details of the full autonomous system. They obtain their information from a designated router, in this example—router 3.

So, router 1 need not exchange routing information with routers 4, 5, and 6, nor does router 2 need to exchange routing information with these routers. The end result is a significant reduction in the amount of routing traffic that is sent through the autonomous system.

Creating Areas

Route Advertising Within the Area

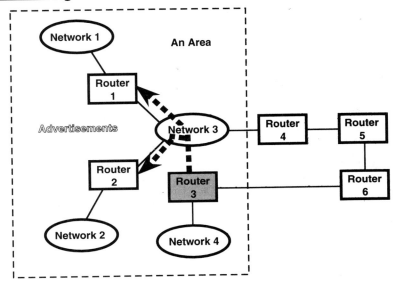

Notes:

_____

_____

_____

_____

_____

_____

The value of partitioning an autonomous system into smaller and more manageable areas is especially important for an enterprise that is faced with the interconnection of a large set of networks, routers, and host computers. It is not unusual for an organization to connect hundreds of networks and thousands of computers together to form an autonomous system.

To illustrate, consider networks 1 and 3 and router 1. Router 1 connects the two networks, network 1 and network 3. Network 1 could take the form of an Ethernet LAN and a host computer supporting workstations, terminals, and servers. Network 3 could take the form of a token ring LAN supporting workstations and terminals.

OSPF requires that one router be assigned the *designated router* for a network. In this manner, the hosts do not have to be concerned with route advertising. In this example, router 1 assumes the responsibility for this task for network 1 and network 3.

Of course, the role of the designated router for network 1 is straightforward, since router 1 is the only router connected to this network.

The assignment of a designated router is accomplished by the use of Hello packets, discussed later. On a specific subnet, the first router that is configured and brought up becomes the designated router. The next router that is brought up becomes the backup designated router. If the designated router fails, the designated backup router takes over.

Next, a process is invoked to elect a new designated backup router among the other routers. Each router on a subnet is assigned a router priority value (0–127), and this value is used to determine the order of selection for the designated backup router.

Designated Routers

Network 1

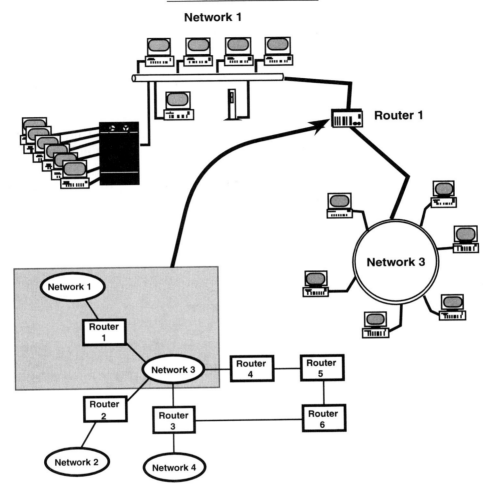

Notes:

_____

_____

_____

In most of the previous discussions on OSPF, we have been using point-to-point router types, where a router only maintains a peer relationship with the routers connected to it on the links. Indeed, a router may only have one peer relationship. With a broadcast network (Ethernet, FDDI, token ring, etc.), a router might have a peer relationship with all routers on the network, resulting in increased overhead in hellos, LSAs, and other operations. With n OSPF routers, there are n × (n − 1)/2 potential peer pairs, which can translate into substantial overhead.

In this illustration, Figure (a) has six routers placed on a subnet. The potential peer relationships are (6 × (5 − 1)/2 = 15, as depicted in Figure (b).

The commonsense approach is to reduce the number of peer relationships, shown in the next figure.

Router Neighbor Pairs

(a) Six routers on the net

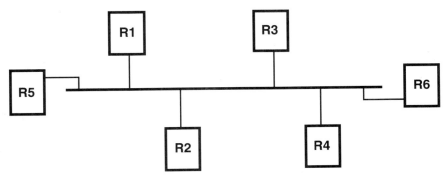

(b) n x (n -1) /2 neighbor pairs

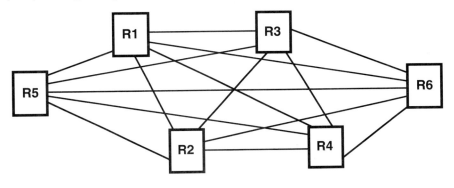

Notes:

_____

_____

_____

_____

_____

OSPF's use of the designated router means the other routers do not have to communicate with each other as far as exchanging hellos, downloading link state databases, and updating LSAs. In Figure (c), the peering relationship is reduced to n − 1 (or 5). R1, R2, R3, R4, and R6 keep their information updated and the databases synchronized with R5, the designated router.

This arrangement is much more efficient than a fully meshed set up, but it means the system is more vulnerable to failure. If problems occur at R5, they affect the other routers.

This is where the aforementioned designated router becomes important. As shown in Figure (d), R6 is the designated router, and all routers establish peer relationships with both R5 and R6. These other routers must synchronize their link state databases with the designated router and the backup designated router.

Router Neighbor Pairs

(Continued)

(c) n -1 neighbor pairs

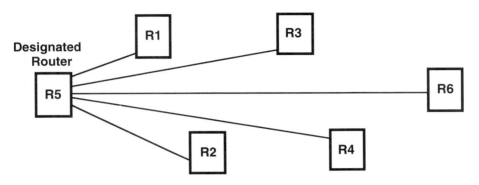

(d) With the designated backup

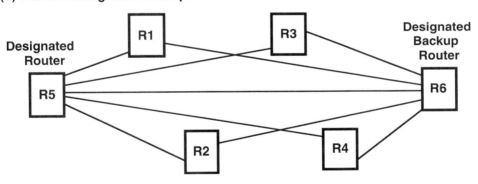

Notes:

_____

_____

_____

_____

OSPF uses another IP multicast address to identify designated routers, including the backup router. It is AllDRouters with a value of 224.0.0.6. In this figure, R2 sends an update LSA onto the network. It has installed this LSA in its link state database and wishes to synchronize this change with the other OSPF routers.

In event 1, the LSA advertisement is multicasted to R5 and R6 with the AllDRouters address. The other routers ignore this message. R5 and R6 receive the information and update their databases. In event 2, R5 floods this LSA to all the routers by placing the AllSPFRouters (224.0.0.5) in the destination address. These routers use the LSA to update their databases.

R6 does not flood the LSA again. After all, R5 has already sent it. But R6 is acting as a watchdog over the process, and if R5 does not send the LSA within a configured interval (a few seconds), R5 will flood this LSA onto the subnet. In this manner, the chances are good that all routers receive the update.

Flooding an Advertisement

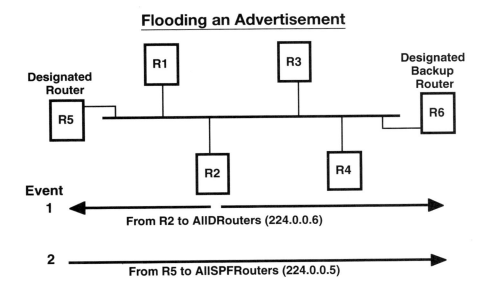

Event
1   From R2 to AllDRouters (224.0.0.6)

2   From R5 to AllSPFRouters (224.0.0.5)

Notes:

_____

_____

_____

_____

_____

_____

Notes:

_____

_____

_____

_____

_____

_____

Summary

- OSPF is the preferred routing protocol in large domains

- Link state advertisements (LSAs) can use different metrics

- Areas are used to contain packet advertisements

- Considerable thought has been given to keeping overhead down

Lecture 14

OSPF Operations

Major Topics

- Establishing link costs (metrics)

- Pruning the tree

We know that each output link at each router has a value assigned to it that represents a metric (or some combination of the TOS parameters). This value can be established by the network administrator. It is technically possible to establish link costs dynamically, based on queue lengths, delays encountered at the routers, and other performance criteria. However dynamic metrics are difficult to manage, and they are not used in connectionless networks like IP or Ethernet. Connection-oriented networks, such as ATM, can use dynamic metrics very effectively because bandwidth is set up for each connection, and OSPF can be used for ongoing advertisements. Once a connection is set up, it stays on a static route (unless a problem occurs). Another user might request an identical connection a short time later, and during this time, OSPF may have found a better route. So, the second customer might have a different path.

Costs are also associated with the other networks that do not belong to this autonomous system. These costs are made available through an External Gateway Protocol.

The lower the cost, the better. This means those interfaces that advertise a low cost are more likely to be used for the relaying of traffic. But it is the sum of all link costs between any two nodes that actually determines how the traffic is routed through the Internet.

Notice that there are no values associated with the output side of a network or a host. These interfaces are considered to have a cost of 0. A designated router that is attached to the network assumes the responsibility of generating the link state advertisements for the network. Therefore, only routers can generate link state advertisements—networks and hosts cannot advertise.

Establishing Link Cost

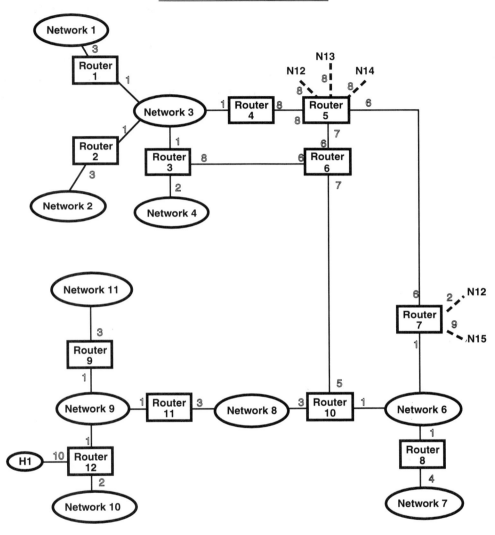

Notes:

_____

_____

The routing table reflects the "pruned" tree of the network. For example, from the perspective of router 6, the network topology appears as shown here.

The costs of the router links going toward router 6 are not relevant and are therefore not shown in the tree, nor are they reflected in the routing table. Only the router links directed toward the destinations from router 6 are used by router 6 in its calculations. This concept is called a *directed graph*.

The "Pruned" Tree as Viewed by Router 6

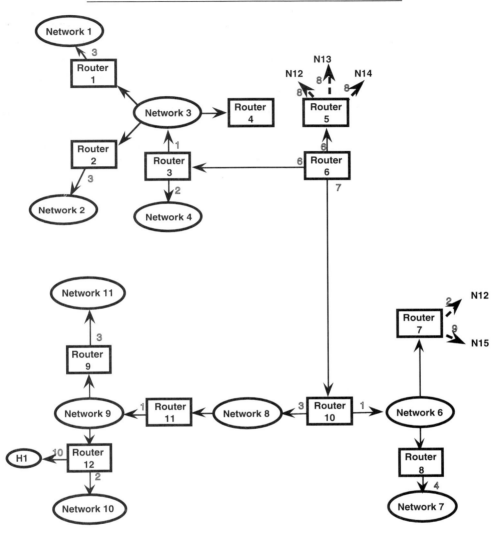

Notes:

_____

_____

Each router now has its own routing database, which reflects its spanning tree—calculated with each router as the reference point, or root.

The routing table for router 6 lists each destination address, the next router that is to receive the traffic—the next node—and the total "distance" from router 6 to the destination. The term *distance* does not mean a physical distance but the sum of the link state costs of the output link of each router in the path to the destination.

Let's see how the table can be used to route traffic. We will assume that router 6 has received a datagram with a destination address for network 7. For our illustration, we will also assume that one spanning tree for router 6 has been calculated—the one presented in this example.

The routing table reveals that the next node to receive the datagram is router 10, and that the total distance to network 7 is 12.

Destination is Network 7

Destination	Next Hop	Distance
N1	Router 3	10
N2	Router 3	10
N3	Router 3	7
N4	Router 3	8
N6	Router 10	8
N7	Router 10	12
N8	Router 10	10
N9	Router 10	11
N10	Router 10	13
N11	Router 10	14
N12	Router 10	10
N13	Router 5	14
N14	Router 5	14
N15	Router 10	17
Host 1	Router 10	21
Router 5	Router 5	6
Router 7	Router 10	8

Notes:

_____

_____

_____

_____

_____

_____

This route is chosen because the cost from router 6 to router 10 is 7, the cost from router 10 to router 8—going through network 6—is 1; and the cost from router 8 to network 7 is 4. So, 7 plus 1 plus 4 equal the total end-to-end distance from router 6 to network 7 of 12.

Similar examinations of the other paths to the destinations from router 6 will sum to the total distance values in router 6's routing table.

The Path to Network 7

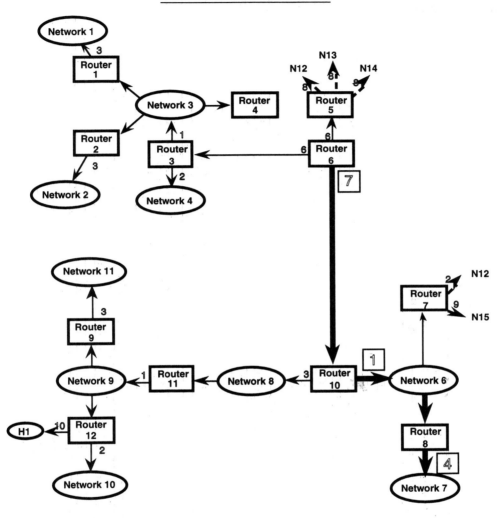

Notes:
_____

_____

_____

Here is the routing entry for the route from router 6 to network 7, as a result of the OSPF spanning tree operations.

Result of the OSPF Spanning Tree

Destination	Route Mask or Prefix	Next Hop	If Index (port)	Metric	Route Type	Source of Route	Route Age	Route Information	MTU
N7	—	R 10	3	12	R	OSPF	—	—	—

Notes:

_____

_____

_____

_____

_____

_____

Notes:

_____

_____

_____

_____

_____

_____

Summary

- Link costs (metrics) are assigned to each interface

- Pruning the tree is performed with spanning tree

Lecture 15

IS-IS (Intermediate System–to– Intermediate System)

Major Topics

- Review of major OSI-based routing specifications

Even though the subject of this chapter is focused on the IS-IS route discovery protocol, IS-IS is only one part of the OSI internetworking suite of protocols. Several internetworking specifications/standards are defined to operate with IS-IS. The standards that have received the most attention are briefly summarized here. Several are explained in more detail in this chapter.

The ISO 8348 standard describes a connection-oriented network service (CONS) with an X.25 packet layer protocol (PLP). For this course, it is of limited interest. Likewise, the ISO 8881, which specifies the use of X.25 in a LAN station attached to a local area network or a packet switched data network, is not covered in this course. ISO 8208 specifies the use of X.25 packet level procedures (PLP) for direct DTE-to-DTE communications, and ISO 8880 part 2 describes the provision and support of connection mode network service,

However, ISO 8473 specifies a connectionless internetworking protocol either with connection-oriented or connectionless subnetworks, and is quite similar to the Internet's Internet Protocol (IP). It is used in OSI-based networks, and complements the Intermediate System-to-Intermediate System (IS-IS) protocol.

In addition, the IS-IS routing exchange protocol (route discovery), published as ISO DP 10589, is of keen interest to this class, as is the End System-to-Intermediate System (ES-IS) protocol important to this course.

<u>OSI Internetworking Protocols</u>

- ISO DP 10589: IS-to-IS (IS-IS) (IS = router)

- ISO 9542: ES-to-IS (ES-IS) (ES = end system)

- ISO 8473: An IP-like protocol

Notes:

_____

_____

_____

_____

_____

_____

OSI has built its network architecture, addressing syntax, and routing operations on a hierarchical concept that is illustrated in this figure. The hierarchical aspect of routing has long proved its worth in both data and voice networks.

This figure shows the lowest level of identification and addressing, which is called level 1 routing. The machines (level 1 routers) are responsible for conveying (a) the traffic directly to end nodes attached to them (such as workstations), or (b) the traffic to other routers for the relaying of the traffic outside their "jurisdiction." This jurisdiction as shown in figure (a) is called an *area*. Level 1 routers route traffic based on one part of an OSI address, called the *ID field*.

The next level of hierarchy, in which level 2 routers relay traffic between areas, is called *inter-area routing*. The systematic organization of multiple areas that communicate with each other through the level 2 routers is called a *routing domain*. In figure (b), level 2 routers are employed to receive the traffic from level 1 routers and determine the appropriate route to the next area.

Finally, a systematized conglomeration of areas can be further organized into a confederation, which is more commonly called *inter-domain routing*. This concept is shown in Figure (c).

OSI Network Hierarchy

(a) Routing domains and areas

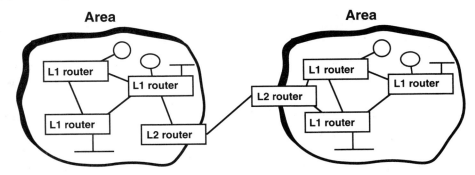

(b) Interdomain (Confederation)

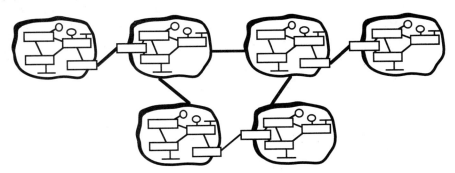

Notes:

_____

_____

_____

_____

_____

Before a detailed analysis is made of the Intermediate System-to-Intermediate System (IS-IS) route discovery protocol, it should prove helpful to compare some terms between the Open Shortest Path First (OSPF) route discovery protocol and IS-IS. First, an OSPF backbone is called a level 2 network in IS-IS. It follows, then, that an OSPF backbone router is called a level 2 router in IS-IS. Next, an OSPF internal router is called a level 1 router in IS-IS.

The IS-IS protocol does not use the term *autonomous system,* which is employed by OSPF. The IS-IS equivalent term is called a *domain.* In addition, the OSPF router that is responsible for route discovery to other autonomous systems is called an *autonomous system boundary router.* IS-IS uses the term *inter-domain router* to define this type of operation.

An IS-IS packet that contains routing information is called a *link state packet* (LSP). In OSPF, this packet is called *a link state advertisement* (LSA).

Finally, an endnode in IS-IS is called a *stub* in OSPF. These devices do not perform route-through operations.

IS-IS and OSPF Terms

IS-IS	OSPF
Level 2	Backbone
Level 2 router	Backbone router
Level 1 router	Internal router
Domain	Autonomous System (AS)
Interdomain router	AS boundary router
Link state packet (LSP)	Link state advertisement (LSA)
Endnode	Stub

Notes:

_____

_____

_____

_____

_____

Notes:

_____

_____

_____

_____

_____

_____

Summary

- OSI routing standards are implemented in several countries and in several protocol suites

- Routing domains are used to manage advertisements

- ISO 8473 (CLNP) is similar to IP

- IS-IS and OSPF are also similar

- ES-IS is used to discover nodes on LANs

Lecture 16

BGP Basics

Major Topics

- Major attributes of BGP

- BGP links and path tree

- Routing operations

- The BGP messages

Even though BGP is a distance-vector protocol, it has several advantages over a conventional distance-vector protocol, such as RIP.

First, BGP sends messages only if something changes and not on a continuous basis. Obviously, this procedure keeps the overhead down on the link.

Second, BGP runs over TCP, which means the BGP messages are delivered in a reliable manner. TCP takes care of error-checking and re-transmitting erred data units.

Third, BGP is able to select a loop-free path even though the system may contain physical loops.

Fourth, BGP stores backup paths, and in the event of failure of the primary path, it need not count-to-infinity while waiting for the network routing tables to stabilize.

Fifth, routing decisions can be based on policy considerations, and need not be based just on the fewest number of hops; that is, BGP does not use metrics. This fifth point is important for public networks, like the Internet, in which the ISPs enter into peering arrangements with each other. These arrangements can be supported with BGP routing policies.

Sixth, a BGP router enters into a relationship with another BFP router through manual configurations and not automatically. This is also important in the Internet to support or deny peering arrangements.

Major Attributes of BGP

- Runs over TCP

- Prevents traffic looping in a looped topology

- Distance-vector, modified by policy decisions

- Immediate adjustment to a failed link or node

Notes:

_____

_____

_____

_____

_____

_____

The Border Gateway Protocol (BGP) is an inter-autonomous system protocol and is a relatively new addition to the family of route discovery protocols (it has seen use since 1989, but not extensively until the last few years). Today, it is the principal route advertising protocol used in the Internet for external gateway operations.

BGP has a number of significant advantages over its predecessor, the External Gateway Protocol (EGP). First, it can operate with networks with looped topologies. Second, as a result of this full advertising, a node that receives more than one possible path (in advertisements) to a destination can, without ambiguity, choose the best path. Third, BGP supports CIDR and address aggregation.

In addition, BGP does not care what type of intra-autonomous route discovery protocol is used. It does not care if multiple intra-autonomous protocols are employed.

BGP is designed to run with a reliable transport layer protocol, such as TCP. Therefore, an implementer of BGP need not be concerned about reliable receipt of traffic, segmentation, etc. These potential problems are handled by the transport layer.

BGP operates by building a graph of ASs. The graph is derived from the routing information exchanged by the BGP routers in the ASs. BGP considers the entire Internet as a graph of ASs with each identified by an AS number (obtained from the Internet). The graph between the ASs is also called a *tree*.

BGP AS Links and Path Tree

A BGP Path Tree:

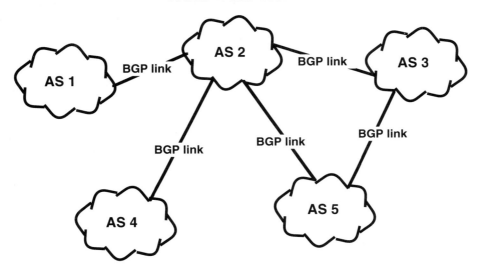

Where:
  AS   Autonomous System
  BGP   Border Gateway Protocol

Notes:

_____

_____

_____

_____

_____

_____

We mentioned earlier that BGP is a distance-vector protocol, but that it need not adhere strictly to a minimum hop approach. This figure shows why. Routers 1–10 are BGP routers that connect ASs 1–5 together. The topology forms a loop between AS 2, AS 3, and AS 5. Under conventional distance vector protocols, a break in the topology, say between router 1 and router 2, would invoke the count to infinity procedure between routers 4, 5, 6, 7, 9, and 10.

BGP knows better. It has discovered that the prefix 192.169.0.0/24 is reachable through AS 1. AS 2 knows that it is in the path to the address, so it would reject any message that had AS 2 in the advertisement.

Furthermore, let us assume that the link between routers 4 and 9 fails. In this situation, AS 5 knows of another path to the AS 1 and can make an immediate recovery. However, keep in mind that AS 5, because of policy decisions, may be prevented from using a path, regardless of the number of hops to the desired destination.

BGP Advertising

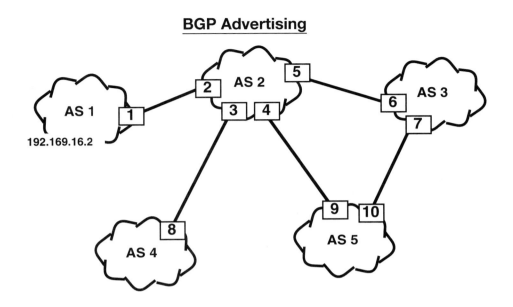

• AS 1 advertises:	192.169.0.0/16	AS 1		
• AS 2 advertises:	192.169.0.0/16	AS 1	AS2	
• AS 3 advertises:	192.169.0.0/16	AS 1	AS2	AS 3
• AS 4 sees:	192.169.0.0/16	AS 1	AS2	
• AS 5 sees:	192.169.0.0/16	AS 1	AS2	
• AS 5 also sees:	192.169.0.0/16	AS 1	AS2	AS 3

Like other routing protocols, BGP uses the concept of a stub. The stub is a network that does not pass-through traffic; it acts as a source and sink for the traffic (it sends or receives traffic). In this figure, the customer network is a stub.

It has been noted in this course that an External Gateway Protocol (EGP) is designed to operate between autonomous systems (AS), and an internal gateway protocol operates within an autonomous system (AS). But what about the operations between an AS (say, an ISP) and a customer? Three methods are used to support this interface, shown in this figure [HALA97].[1]

In figure (a), BGP is deployed between the customer and the service provider (An ISP that is assigned as AS number). In this situation, BGP is called the external BGP (EBGP). It is so-named because BGP can operate between ASs or within an AS. As discussed later, an internal BGP (IBGP) is used to tunnel a user's traffic through a transit (pass-through) AS. For this operation, the provider gives the customer a private AS number (65412-65535), but uses the provider's AS number for its operations beyond the provider-customer interface.

In figure (b), an IGP is deployed between the customer and the service provider. In this situation, the customer uses RIP, OSPF, etc. to advertise its addresses to the service provider. This operation is done by agreements between the two parties. As examples, conventional prefix advertising may be performed, or the customer may use the ISP's address space, and the two may use the Network Address Translation (NAT) protocol for the non-global address to global address translation.

In figure (c), the customer has static (preconfigured) routes to the provider. After all, the customer's network is a stub, and there is only one way into and out of the stub. This interface can also be supported by NAT.

---

[1][HALA97] Halabi, Bassam, *Internet Routing Architectures,* Cisco Press, New Riders Publishing, 1997.

How the Customer is Supported

(a) With External BGP

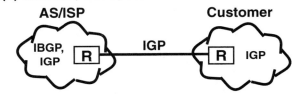

(b) With RIP, OSPF, etc.

(c) Or pre-configured

Notes:

_____

_____

_____

_____

_____

_____

BGP uses four different types of messages for its operations. They are:

- **Open:** Used to establish neighbors (BGP peers). This operation must occur before any advertising can take place.
- **Update:** Used to exchange addresses and routing information. This message contains three major fields. First, the network layer reachability information (NLRI) advertises networks (with the IP prefix, for classless routing). The BGP node uses this information to inform its neighbors about its other BGP neighbors. Second, withdrawn or unfeasible routes can be advertised. Third, path attributes are used to keep track of items such as route preference, next hop, and aggregation information.
- **Notification:** Used when an error occurs, or a peer connection is closed.
- **Keepalive:** Used between peers to make sure the peers are up and running and the link to them is operational.

The BGP Messages

- Open: Used to establish neighbors (BGP peers)

- Update: Used to exchange addresses and routing information
    1. Network layer reachability information (NLRI)
    2. Withdrawn/unfeasible routes
    3. Path attributes

- Notification: Used when an error occurs, or a peer connection is closed

- Keepalive: Makes sure peer is up,
  and link is operational

Notes:

_____

_____

_____

_____

_____

_____

Notes:

_____

_____

_____

_____

_____

_____

Summary

- BGP is used extensively in the Internet, between Autonomous Systems (ASs)

- Based on minimum hop and policy decisions

Lecture 17

BGP Operations

Major Topics

- Non-transit and transit Autonomous Systems

- Routing Confederations

- Route Reflectors

One valuable aspect of the BGP and AS concept is the transit network or transit AS (which was introduced earlier). The idea is shown in this figure.

An AS need not originate and terminate all traffic that flows through it. This AS is a multihomed transit network. The term *multihomed* means that the AS has more than one interface to other ASs, hosts, and/or networks. The term *transit* means the traffic has a source or destination address outside the AS. Therefore, the term *nontransit* means that the AS does not permit traffic not destined for the AS (or not originated in the AS) to pass through it.

Some Internets/intranets permit transit operations, and some do not. The decision to permit transit traffic to pass through an organization's AS is based on the organization's routing policy.

This figure shows an example of a multihomed, non-transit AS, which is AS 1, and ISP A. AS 1 advertises addresses for NW1 and NW2 to AS 2 and AS 3. AS 2 and AS 3 advertise NW3, NW4 and NW5, NW6 respectively to AS 1.

AS 1 does not relay the respective advertisements of AS 2 and AS 3 farther than its own AS. Consequently, AS 2 and AS 3 do not know they can reach each other through AS 1, and will not relay traffic to AS 1 for the networks that reside in these two autonomous systems.

Multihomed Non-Transit
Autonomous System (AS)

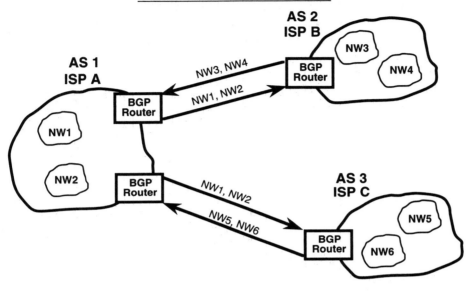

Where:
  BGP   Border Gateway Protocol
  ISP   Internet service provider
  NW   Network

Notes:

_____

_____

_____

_____

_____

_____

This figure shows a transit multihomed AS. This AS relays traffic through it—that is, traffic that does not originate nor terminate in the AS. The figure also shows two other aspects of multihomed transit ASs. The BGP operation that exchanges advertisements between the autonomous systems is called an *external BGP,* or *EBGP.* The routers that operate at this interface are called *border routers.*

The advertisements are also carried through AS 1 to allow AS 2 and AS 3 to inform each other about their networks. This BGP operation is called an *internal BGP,* or *IBGP.* The routers that exchange this information are called *transit routers.*

Multihomed Transit
Autonomous System (AS)

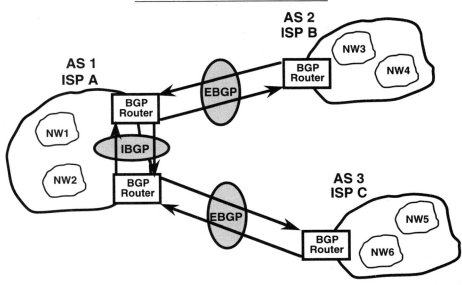

Where:
  BGP   Border Gateway Protocol
  EBGP   External BGP
  IBGP   Internal BGP
  ISP   Internet service provider
  NW   Network

Notes:

To continue the discussion on multihomed transit autonomous systems, this figure shows how the route advertisements are conveyed by AS 1 to AS 2 and AS 3. The fact that AS 1 is advertising on behalf of AS 2 and AS 3 means that AS 1 agrees to be a transit network for AS 2 and AS 3.

The transit routers in AS 1 are also connected to non-transit routers in the autonomous system. The non-transit routers need not be configured with BGP, but can use an internal gateway protocol (IGP) such as OSPF.

Multihomed Transit
Autonomous System (AS)

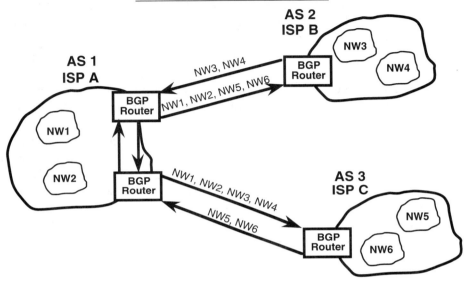

Where:
   BGP   Border Gateway Protocol
   EBGP   External BGP
   IBGP   Internal BGP
   ISP   Internet service provider
   NW   Network

Notes:

_____

_____

_____

_____

_____

As large enterprises, such as ISPs, become even larger, one autonomous system can become unwieldy. The IBGP configurations can become quite complex, and a router may have to support many internal BGP sessions. One method to deal with this problem is to "divide and conquer"—break the AS down into smaller parts.

An autonomous system can be divided into multiple autonomous systems and grouped into a single confederation. To the outside, this partitioning is transparent, and the divided ASs appear as one autonomous system. This figure shows the idea of the routing domain configuration.

Each of the autonomous systems is fully meshed within itself, and has connections to the other ASs in the confederation. The peers in the different autonomous systems have EBGP sessions, but they exchange routing information as IBGP peers, and the conventional rules for IBGP are in effect. Several key router configuration parameters are used to enable one IGP to be used within the confederation.

Notice that EBGP is operating between the ASs in the confederation. This configuration is needed because each AS uses a unique AS number, and thus the EBGP routing packets are used.

A Routing Domain Confederation

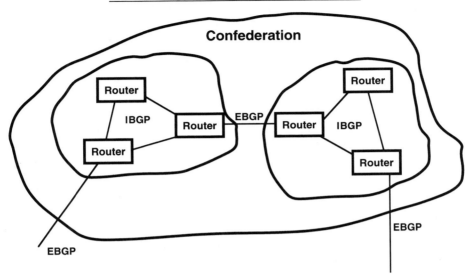

Notes:

_____

_____

_____

_____

_____

_____

Another approach to combat the scaling problem is to configure the routers to support a route reflector. This operation means that all IBGP speakers do not have to be fully meshed. The approach is depicted in this figure. Router 2 is configured to be a route reflector, and assumes the responsibility for passing the routing information to a set (or one) of IBGP neighbors. When router 2 receives the routing information from router 1, it advertises the information to router 3 . Router 3 then "reflects" the routing information to router 4. Thus, IBGP sessions between router 2 and router 4 are unnecessary.

This simple example may not show the savings in routing sessions through the use of the router reflector. But consider that router 2 might have IBGP sessions with hundreds of other routers, and the reflector helps reduce the overhead of these many sessions. To see why, we need some more information. Internal BGP peers of the route reflector are divided into: (a) client peers, and (b) nonclient peers. The route reflector forms an association with its client peers called a *cluster,* and these routers do not have to be fully meshed with each other. They do *not* communicate with IBGP speakers that are outside the cluster.

To demonstrate the reflector operations, consider that when a route reflector receives routing information, it performs the following operations:

- It advertises the external BGP information to all clients and non-client peers
- Any information from a nonclient peer is advertised to all clients
- A route from a client is advertised to all clients and nonclient peers, which means the clients do not have to be fully meshed

The Route Reflector

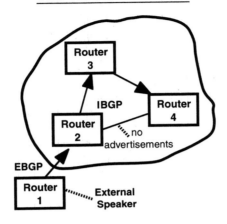

Notes:

_____

_____

_____

_____

_____

_____

Notes:

_____

_____

_____

_____

_____

_____

Summary

- Non-transit and transit ASs control pass-throughs

- Routing Confederations and Route Reflectors
  help with potential overload problems

Lecture 18

PNNI

Major Topics

- Characteristics of PNNI

- The layers of PNNI

- Example of a PNNI topology

One can reasonably ask why yet another set of specifications is required
to define another protocol in the ATM environment. Indeed, for the ATM
implementer or the user of the ATM equipment, the proliferation of new
specifications creates more complexity in a network (the PNNI specification by itself is 365 pages in length). But, PNNI is published for a very
good reason. The ITU-T does not concern itself with the operations of private networks. (From the ITU-T perspective, the Internet is considered
to be a private network.) Additionally, the ITU-T does not concern itself
with the distribution of routing information, route discovery nor topology
analysis (except for some of the newer SS7 protocols). These operations
have been left to the implementation of individual telecommunications
administrations.

This approach is not the case with PNNI. The PNNI philosophy is
that these important considerations cannot be left to individual implementations. For full interworking to occur between ATM-based networks
and ATM switches, there must be standards involved in defining how information is distributed between switches in an ATM network. Thus,
PNNI consists of two major parts. The first part defines a protocol to exchange routing information for route discovery. It defines the operations
for the distribution of topology and routing information between ATM
switches. It allows the switches to compute paths through a network.
The second part of PNNI is used for signaling, and defines the procedures to establish point-to-point or point-to-multipoint connections
through an ATM network. In this regard, the PNNI signaling operations
are quite similar to many of the other protocols, because they are based
on the ITU-T Q.2931 specification.

Characteristics of the Private
Network-to-Network Interface (PNNI)

- Organized into (a) route discovery, and (b) signaling

- Route discovery:

    Based on research from Internet activities

    Uses OSPF (Open Shortest Path First) concepts

    Advertises metrics based on ATM services

- Signaling:

    Derived from ITU-T Q.2931
    . . . . with some added features

Notes:

_____

_____

_____

_____

_____

The PNNI model is depicted in this figure, which obviously is almost identical to the NNI signaling stack defined by other standards organizations. One difference pertains to the PNNI call control and PNNI protocol control. The call control layer services the upper layers for functions such as routing, routing exchange, and allocation of resources. The PNNI protocol control layer rests below the call control layer and thus provides services to call control. The PNNI call control layer is responsible for processing the signaling. It operates with state machines for the incoming and outgoing calls. The layers below these two layers are based on the ITU-T Q.2xxx specifications.

The PNNI Layers

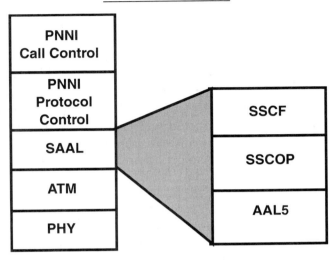

Where:
  AAL   ATM adaptation layer
  SAAL   Signaling ATM adaptation layer
  SSCF   Service specific coordination function
  SSCOP   Service specific connection oriented protocol

Notes:

_____

_____

_____

_____

_____

_____

The PNNI architecture is based on a hierarchical structure. Nodes are associated with level in a hierarchy, and nodes that belong to the same hierarchy are in the same peer group. An example of the PNNI hierarchy is provided in this figure, which I have derived from the ATM Forum PNNI specification. The numbers and alphanumerics in this figure represent addresses. They are drawn in place of specific addresses for ease of explanation. The highest hierarchy of this figure is peer group A, identified with the address of A. The nodes inside the group are identified as A1, A4, etc. and they are connected with logical links. Within each peer group is a peer group leader whose responsibility is to receive topology information from all nodes in the group and advertise this information to other groups. The information that is advertised is "filtered" in that summary information and is given to the other groups.

The next level of the PNNI hierarchy is shown with peer groups A.1, A.2, and so on. Within these peer groups are other nodes labeled as A.1.3, A.4.1, etc. PNNI establishes rules about how messages can be sent up and down the hierarchy, based on the functions of the nodes in a peer group. Once again, this concept is designed to place restrictions on how many route advertisements can be sent between nodes.

The PNNI Hierarchy

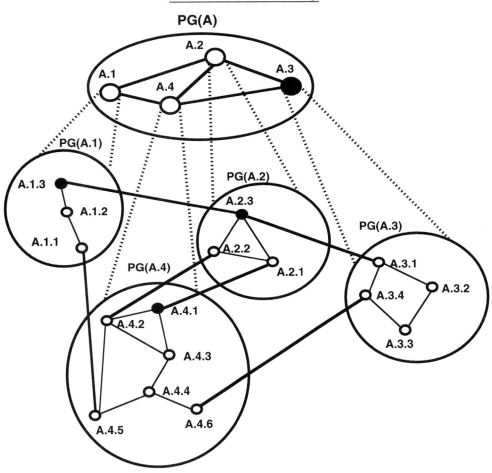

Notes:

_____

_____

_____

_____

_____

_____

Summary

- PNNI is designed for ATM networks

- Its use is limited at this time

Lecture 19

Routing in Mobile Networks

Major Topics

- The IP "attachment" address

- The Mobile IP Protocol

- Address advertisements with Mobile IP

The purpose of Mobile IP is to enhance the conventional Internet protocols to support the roaming of nodes, wherein the mobile station can receive datagrams no matter where they are located. Without the use of Mobile IP, a mobile station node would have to change its IP address whenever it moves to a new network (that is, whenever it changes its point of attachment). Additionally, without the use of Mobile IP, routes specific to the host would have to be propagated into the networks that are concerned with supporting this host. Obviously, these two operations are not efficient and would create tremendous housekeeping problems for the network. In addition, the nature in which IP addresses are used to identify higher-layer connections (sockets to the applications themselves) makes it an impossible task to maintain this relationship if the IP address changes.

The requirements for any type of system that supports the mobility of an IP node are summarized here:

- The mobile station must be able to communicate when it moves to another point of attachment without having to change its IP address.
- The mobile station must be able to communicate with non mobile-IP nodes. This should require no enhancements to conventional hosts or routers.
- Authentication must be provided to protect against security breaches.
- Overhead traffic flowing across the air interface must be kept to a minimum in order to reduce complexity and cut down on the power requirements for "continuous" transmission of overhead messages.
- The IP address must be the conventional IP address currently used in internets.
- There must be no additional requirements for these procedures (for example, the allocation of special addresses).
- Mobile IP supports mobility in wireless, as well as wire-based, networks.

Mobile IP

- The mobile station keeps permanent address

- Transparently sends and receive datagrams

- No changes to Internet routing tables

Notes:

_____

_____

_____

_____

_____

_____

The IP address is a fixed, point-of-attachment address. The address has a network/subnetwork value and a host value. The host value is associated with the network/subnetwork value. In Figure (a) an MS with address 192.168.2.1 is attached to the IWF with address 192.168.2.0. It sends a datagram to host 192.168.1.1 that is attached to the IWF with address 192.168.1.0. The contents of the addresses in this datagram are shown on the right side of the figure. SA mean source address, and DA means destination address.

In Figure (b) the operation is reversed with host 192.168.1.1 sending a datagram to MS 192.168.2.1. Thus far, the operations are straightforward, and the flow of traffic is the same as if the MS were a fixed host.

Initial Set Up

(a) From MS to other host

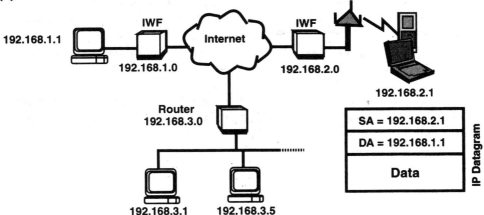

(b) From other host to MS

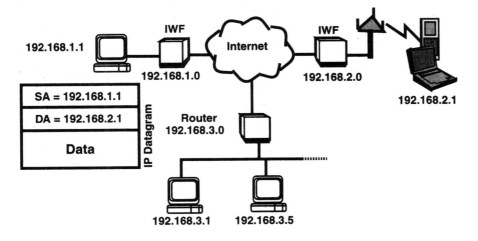

Notes:

_____

_____

The problem occurs when the mobile station (called a mobile wireless data terminal, or mobile node [MN]) moves to a different network. In Figure (c), the mobile user has moved to network 192.16.3.0 and is assigned address 192.168.3.2. Host 192.168.1.1 is not aware of the transit and continues to send datagrams to the mobile user's old address. The result, of course, is that the home IWF (192.168.2.0) cannot deliver the traffic, in which case it discards it, and maybe sends back to the originator an ICMP error message of "destination unreachable."

Even though traffic cannot be delivered to the transit machine, it can still send datagrams correctly. So, it is a one-way problem: the inability for the transit user to receive traffic.

The Mobile Station Moves

(c) From host to transit host

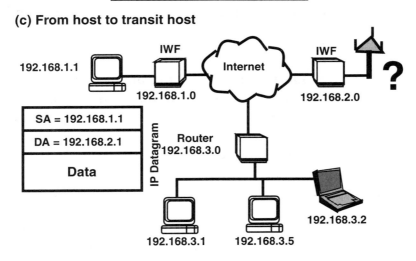

Notes:

_____

_____

_____

_____

_____

_____

The top part of this figure is a simplified version of earlier illustrations. The bottom part is a more detailed view of the advertisement and registration operations.

The legend for this figure is:

SA   Source address in the IP datagram header
DA   Destination address in the IP datagram header
COA   Care of address
MN   Mobile node
HA   Home agent address
FA   Foreign agent address
MNHA   Mobile node home address (permanent address)

In event 1, foreign agent B sends an agent advertisement message, which is broadcast out onto the subnet. The IP destination address (DA) is set to 255.255.255.255. Notice that the advertisement contains a list of care of addresses, from which a mobile node can pick. The advertisement also contains a field that identifies the advertiser as a foreign agent.

In event 2, the mobile node responds with a registration request message. The IP source address (SA) and destination address (DA) identify the mobile node A and foreign agent B, respectively. The mobile node has chosen COA 192.168.3.2 and has provided its home address in the body of the advertisement.

After altering some of the fields in the IP header and the registration request message (in event 2a), foreign agent B sends this advertisement to home agent C. The IP source address now contains the address of foreign agent B, and the IP destination address contains the address of home agent C.

The Registration Activities: The Request

(see left page for legend)

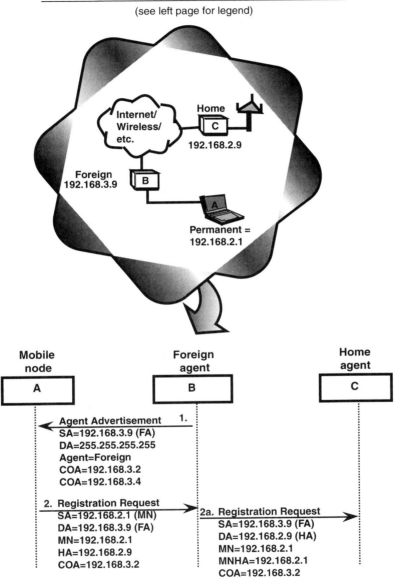

Mobile node

Foreign agent

Home agent

A

B

C

1.
← Agent Advertisement
SA=192.168.3.9 (FA)
DA=255.255.255.255
Agent=Foreign
COA=192.168.3.2
COA=192.168.3.4

2. Registration Request →
SA=192.168.2.1 (MN)
DA=192.168.3.9 (FA)
MN=192.168.2.1
HA=192.168.2.9
COA=192.168.3.2

2a. Registration Request →
SA=192.168.3.9 (FA)
DA=192.168.2.9 (HA)
MN=192.168.2.1
MNHA=192.168.2.1
COA=192.168.3.2

This figure is a continuation of the example of the Mobile IP registration operations.

The legend for this figure is:

SA   Source address in the IP datagram header
DA   Destination address in the IP datagram header
COA   Care of address
MN   Mobile node
HA   Home agent address
FA   Foreign agent address
MNHA Mobile node home address (permanent address)

In event 3, foreign agent C responds to the registration request message it received in event 2. This agent places its address in the IP source address field and foreign agent B's address in the IP destination address field. The addresses in the registration replay message are the mobile node's home address and the address of the home agent.

You might wonder why home agent B's address is coded twice in this reply. First, the Mobile IP message is the data field of the IP datagram and is divorced from the IP header. Second, it may be that the originator of this reply is not the home agent itself, but a server that is acting on behalf of the home agent. Therefore, foreign agent B receives the reply, it would have information about the server and the home agent.

In event 3a, foreign agent B sends the registration reply message to the mobile node after changing the IP source and destination addresses to foreign agent B and mobile node A, respectively.

This completes the bootstrapping operations. Hereafter, traffic can be exchanged between all parties.

The Registration Activities: The Reply

(see left page for legend)

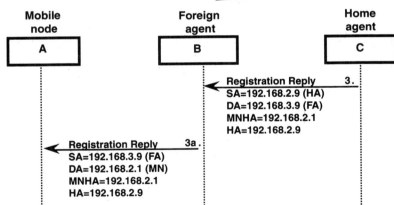

The Registration Activities: The Reply

(see left page for legend)

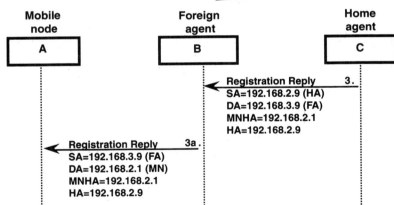

Mobile node	Foreign agent	Home agent
A	B	C

Registration Reply   3.
SA=192.168.2.9 (HA)
DA=192.168.3.9 (FA)
MNHA=192.168.2.1
HA=192.168.2.9

Registration Reply   3a.
SA=192.168.3.9 (FA)
DA=192.168.2.1 (MN)
MNHA=192.168.2.1
HA=192.168.2.9

Notes:

As a result of the operations discussed previously, the agents have set up entries in their address tables. As this figure shows, both agents have stored information about the relationship of mobile node A's permanent address and its care of address. When home agent C receives an IP datagram with DA of 192.168.2.1, it knows that this node is not directly attached to one of C's attached subnets. It also knows that C can be reached at B, through the care of address.

Therefore, based on conventional routing operations, node C consults a routing table to determine how to reach node B. Nodes C and B know about each other through RIP, OSPF, or BGP.

If the mobile node is attached to a local area network (LAN), there will be a LAN Media Access Control (MAC) address associated with the L_3 IP COA, as shown in node B's table.

Address Bindings

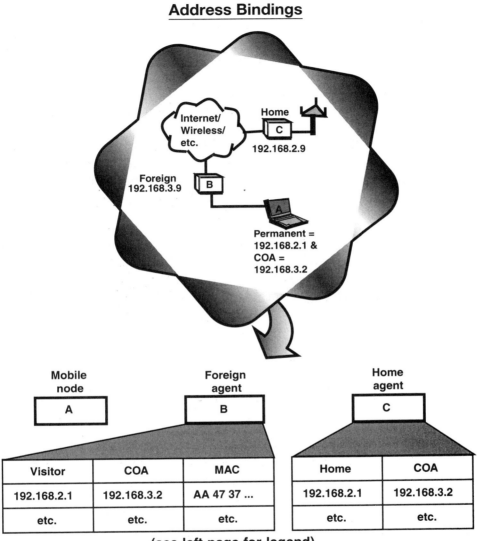

Mobile node				Home agent	
A				C	

Visitor	COA	MAC		Home	COA
192.168.2.1	192.168.3.2	AA 47 37 ...		192.168.2.1	192.168.3.2
etc.	etc.	etc.		etc.	etc.

(see left page for legend)

Notes:

_____

_____

We now have enough information to show how data are exchanged between IP nodes. In so doing, the concept of the Mobile IP tunnel is explained. The term *tunnel* is used synonymously with *encapsulation*. The term *de-tunnel* (a new word for Webster's) is used synonymously with *de-capsulation*.

Once again, recall that one of the purposes of Mobile IP is to allow a mobile node to continue to use its home IP address when it is attached to another subnet.

We also learned that the Mobile IP packet contains two sets of IP addresses. One set identifies the IP addresses of the two communicating hosts. The other set identifies the IP addresses of the tunneling node and the de-tunneling node. This figure shows the idea of the Mobile IP tunnel.

Subnet 192.168.1.0, illustrated in earlier figures, is added to this figure. Host D with IP address 192.168.1.1 on subnet 192.168.1.0 is sending traffic to host A (192.168.2.1), the mobile node. Host D's datagrams are routed to A's home agent, node C. At this node, the tunnel is created, and the datagrams are relayed to foreign agent B. At node B, the tunnel ends, and node B delivers the traffic to node A.

The Mobile IP Tunnel

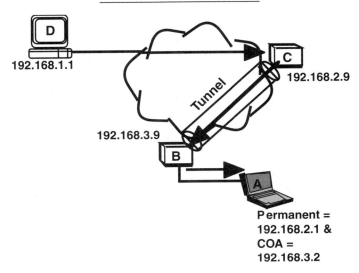

192.168.1.1

192.168.2.9

192.168.3.9

Tunnel

Permanent =
192.168.2.1 &
COA =
192.168.3.2

Notes:

_____

_____

_____

_____

_____

_____

This figure shows an end-to-end operation, with the delivery of datagrams from host D to mobile node A. The figure is numbered with events 1–5 to help you follow this explanation.

Event 1: Host D constructs a datagram with its address in the SA and host D's address in the DA. Through conventional routing operations, the datagram arrives at mobile node A's home agent, node C.

Event 2: Using the binding table created during the registration operations, home agent C correlates mobile node A's permanent address with its COA.

Event 3: To begin the tunneling operations, home agent C builds the second IP header (the external header), containing C's address in the SA, and the COA of mobile node D in the DA. Through conventional routing operations, the datagram arrives at mobile node D's foreign agent, node B. Notice that the IP addresses in the internal header have not been altered.

Event 4: For the de-tunneling operations, node B uses the binding table created during the registration operations, and correlates mobile node A's permanent address with its COA. It knows the DA is a COA attached to node B. It examines the inner IP address DA to find node A's permanent address.

Event 5: After having decapsulated the outer IP header, foreign agent B routes the datagram to node A.

The Mobile IP End-to-End Operations

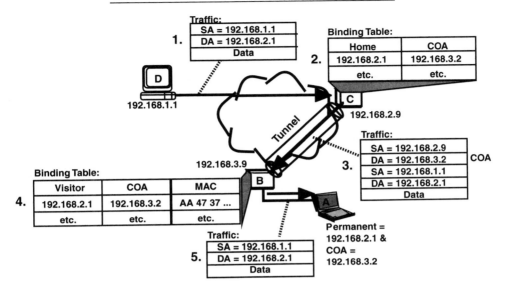

1.

Traffic:

| SA = 192.168.1.1 |
| DA = 192.168.2.1 |
| Data |

Binding Table:

2.

Home	COA
192.168.2.1	192.168.3.2
etc.	etc.

D
192.168.1.1

Tunnel

C
192.168.2.9

3.   **Traffic:**

SA = 192.168.2.9	
DA = 192.168.3.2	COA
SA = 192.168.1.1	
DA = 192.168.2.1	
Data	

192.168.3.9

B

Binding Table:

4.

Visitor	COA	MAC
192.168.2.1	192.168.3.2	AA 47 37 ...
etc.	etc.	etc.

A

Permanent =
192.168.2.1 &
COA =
192.168.3.2

5.   **Traffic:**

| SA = 192.168.1.1 |
| DA = 192.168.2.1 |
| Data |

Notes:

_____

_____

_____

_____

_____

_____

Notes:

_____

_____

_____

_____

_____

_____

Summary

- IP addresses are network/host-specific

- Roaming to other networks was not envisioned

- Mobile IP: Allows an IP address to be used in different networks

Lecture 20

Wrap-Up

Follow Ups to this Program

The accompanying text book as some good
follow up information:

- Configuring routers, see Chapters 5, 6, 7, 8 and
  Appendix D

- Chapter 4 has more details on LAN bridges, and
  for IBM users, information on Data Link Switching

- Page 9: More information on Gateways

- Page 57: Spanning Tree Algorithm

- Page 63: Integrated bridging and routing

Notes:

_____

_____

_____

_____

_____

_____

Wrap-Up

Follow Ups to this Program

- Page 128: Packet containment (OSPF)

- Page 145: OSPF packets

- Page 163: Policy-based routing

- Page 173: BGP packets

- Chapter 8: The Cisco routing protocols

- Appendix D: The Next Hop Resolution Protocol (NHRP), used in ATM backbones